# Miss Cleo's Cayman Kitchen

## Treasured Recipes From East End

By Cleopatra Conolly
with Barbara Currie Dailey

*Published by*
**Island Fever Press Ltd., and Cayman Net Ltd.**
P.O. Box 10707
Grand Cayman KY1-1006
Cayman Islands, BWI.

# Miss Cleo's Cayman Kitchen
## Treasured Recipes from East End

Second Printing 2007
Copyright 2006

ISBN-13:     978-976-95054-3-8 (pbk)
ISBN-10:     976-95054-3-9 (pbk)

The exception, of course, is reproduction of any recipe from this book in your own kitchen. The authors hope this book will inspire every reader to enjoy these timeless recipes and rediscover cooking the way it was in Cayman a long time ago.

The information contained in this book is authentic and complete to the best of our knowledge. All recommendations are made without any guarantees on the part of the authors or publishers. The authors and publishers disclaim all liability in connection with the use of this information and products mentioned.

*Published by*
**Island Fever Press Ltd., and Cayman Net Ltd.**
P.O. Box 10707, Grand Cayman KY1 -1006
CAYMAN ISLANDS


Cover design and layout by Island Fever Press Ltd.,
Grand Cayman, Cayman Islands
Printed by Thompson Press for Cayman Net Ltd.

# $\mathscr{D}$edication

To my dear family and the many
friends I have here in Cayman and
overseas who have become like
family to me. God Bless you all!

-- Cleopatra Conolly

10 8th 2007

To Terri

May you have a Long healthy &

happy life

May God Bless you

Love

Cleo

Miss Cleopatra Conolly

# Miss Cleo's Acknowledgements

First of all, I want to thank my mother, Anna Louise Watson Conolly for the prayer she offered to God, asking Him to provide a job for me with an American family. At that time, it was before Mr. Eric and Mrs. Suzy Bergstrom and the Tortuga Club were around. But I will say that years later, my mother's prayer was answered and I got that job before she died.

I want to thank Mr. Eric and Mrs. Suzy Bergstrom for hiring me when I was 39 and had never worked for anyone outside my home. Suzy, you taught me a lot about foreign foods and I thank you fourfold. Mr. Eric once said that I could cook every food in the world –"except those darn mashed potatoes" which I couldn't' seem to make to his liking.

I went to work at the Tortuga Club in 1964 on a two weeks' trial and ended up working with the Bergstroms for 14 years. Even now, we are still like one big family. I owe more thanks than I can ever put into words to all of them, including the children: Kris, Jimmy, Karie, Sheree and Barrie Sue and their families. I am especially grateful for all their kindness after the Hurricane Ivan. In 2005 they organized the Friends of Miss Cleo, and thanks to Kris and Debi's company Edgewater Construction and donations and volunteer efforts, I moved into a brand new home on September 17, 2005, a year after Hurricane Ivan.

Thanks and love to my brother Frank and his family, who have helped me stay strong throughout my trials and tribulations. I want to give a special prayer of thanks for my nephew Dawson Whittaker, and my niece Ann Kirchman, for taking me into their homes for an entire year after Hurricane Ivan.

I want to thank Mr. David Morritt for making me the Hospitality Ambassador at Morritt's Tortuga Club after I retired from the kitchen after 32 years. I also want to thank the many owners and guests at Tortuga Club and other friends here and overseas who showed me such concern and kindness after Hurricane Ivan.

Finally, I want to thank Barbara Dailey for the many hours she spent helping me write this book. Without her, it would not have been possible. I also want to thank Mr. Desmond Seales for printing the book and for everything he has done to help me and others over the years.

May God Bless you all!
With love,

**Cleopatra Conolly**

Miss Cleo and her brother,
Frank Conolly

# Contents

## Introduction

## Part One:
## Recipes and Memories from Old East End

- Miss Cleo's Story
- Roast Yams and Coconut Rice: Memories of My East End Girlhood
- The Amazing Coconut: A Caymanian Staple
- Old Time East End Cookery & Recipes

## Part Two:
## Miss Cleo's Kitchen: Recipes From Around the World at Tortuga Club

- Introduction: Miss Cleo's International Cuisine at Tortuga Club
- Cleo's Island Cookery Tips
- Appetizers and Drinks
- Homemade Breads
- The Soup Kettle
- Tasty Side Dishes
- Cleo's Conch Recipes
- Cayman Turtle
- Cleo's Wonderful Fish  Recipes
- Seafood Treasures
- Meat Dishes from Around the World
- Delicious Chicken Dishes
- Barbecue and Peppers
- Cleo's Famous Homemade Pies
- Cakes, Desserts and Special Sweets

## Glossary & Index

- Ingredients & Measures
- Index

Barrie Quappe, Miss Cleo and Suzy Soto celebrating at Miss
Cleo's 40th Anniversary at Morritt's Tortuga

David Morrit, owner of Morritt's Tortuga, and Miss Cleo at
the 40th Anniversary celebration

# Introduction
## A Time Capsule of Recipes Rediscovered

*By Barbara Currie Dailey*

This cook book is by no means a complete collection of the many dishes Miss Cleo prepared for guests during her years as executive chef of the Tortuga Club Kitchen. It represents only those recipes she recalls as being visitors' favorites and ones most requested by dining room guests, both foreign and local. Some of these were transcribed from her original handwritten kitchen notes of menus kept in a grade school composition notebook. Others were written from memory after Hurricane Ivan destroyed her house and all of her belongings on September 12, 2004.

In *Miss Cleo's Cayman Kitchen* readers will find a time capsule of recipes worth rediscovering today. There are Caymanian dishes Miss Cleo remembers from growing up in East End and family recipes reconstructed from memory. The second section features a variety of favorite local and international dishes "a la Cleo" dating back to the 1960s that appeared on her Tortuga Club dinner menus.

### A Look at the 1960's Culinary Highlights

When the Tortuga Club opened in 1963, Cayman was an unknown destination and island life was simple---and a daily challenge for most residents. Caymanians considered luxuries many of the amenities people in the United States and others overseas took for granted. In a Caymanian kitchen, a sturdy box grater and pressure cooker were the only "conveniences." There were no well-stocked modern supermarkets as there were in the USA: no Foster's Food Fair, Kirk's Supermarket or Hurley's in Grand Cayman. Fresh imported produce was scarce and dairy products and meats were luxuries imported frozen. Everything was expensive --grocery shopping was a weekly treasure hunt and adventure. An intact head of iceberg lettuce or perfect cabbage from By-Rite in George Town was considered a real prize. In this little country, most home cooks still used every part of everything and prepared simple, delicious meals using what was on hand. The coconut was one of the most important ingredients *and seasonings* in local kitchens. Fresh conch, lobster and fish were still easy to find.

Meanwhile, America was undergoing a culinary revolution. Busy housewives were under the spell of kitchen gadgets and convenience foods like Duncan Hines cake mixes, Velveeta cheese and creamed soups. Cooking with these products was considered exciting and sophisticated. Cans of creamed condensed soups were a homemaker's dream and the secret to everything from Chicken a la King and to lazy gravy substitutes.

At the same time, America's culinary horizons expanded globally. *The New Betty Crocker Picture Cookbook* appeared in the early 1960s, introducing housewives to foreign dishes like Lobster Thermidor and Sukiyaki. Craig Clairborne's best- seller *The New York Times Cookbook* showed Americans that they, too, could prepare an ethnic smorgasbord of recipes at home from countries far away. His columns in the *New York Times* also introduced recipes unknown previously except to wealthy world travelers. Suddenly America was passionate about showy foreign food.

Television programs also fueled curiosity about foreign cuisines. In 1962 PBS television started airing *The French Chef*, bringing Julia Child into millions of homes to teach fine French cuisine—with live demonstrations by the sometimes accident-prone big lady chef, often filled with funny faux pas. America fell in love with things Françoise, and snapped up copies of *Mastering the Art of French Cooking, volumes I and II.*

In spite of all these new tastes and temptations, the North American palate still loved and missed those simple homey comfort foods that required "slow cooking", even as microwaves and a range of gadgets cluttered the kitchen. In a culinary landscape of ever expanding horizons, people still longed for tender braised roasts with velvety gravy, homemade bread (before bread makers) soups, meatloaf, macaroni and cheese, chicken and dumplings, lemon meringue pie and desserts with fanciful names like Snow Pudding and Blueberry Imperial.

Now imagine, 30 or 40 year ago, traveling several thousand miles to a remote resort on a tiny Caribbean island and finding those cherished dishes on the dinner menu, alongside exotic foods like conch, turtle and fresh local seafood! How did Miss Cleo, a 39 year old lady from the most isolated part of Cayman who had never worked outside of home, learn to cook such things and become the island's first female executive chef? It was a combination of guidance from Tortuga Club's owner Suzy Bergstrom; Cleo's own natural "cooking sense", curiosity; patience and hard work. Miss Cleo had only a primary school education but she loved to read. She also enjoyed collecting recipes from magazines and cookbooks sent to her by friends or gathered in her travels overseas, and trying them at the Club. Miss Cleo learned to cook popular recipes of the 1960s and 1970s, adapting those recipes using ingredients available locally and adding her own unique touches.

For foreign visitors –and very quickly, a large number of island residents—the restaurant at Tortuga Club was the source of exciting gourmet discoveries. In her kitchen, Miss Cleo cooked up an adventurous mixture of island dishes alongside her adaptations of sophisticated and foreign comfort foods of the day. Guests cleaned their plates every evening and clamored for an encore.

Today many people here and overseas fondly remember Miss Cleo's Cayman Kitchen and miss her special recipes. Miss Cleo would love to hear from her friends. You can write to her:

**Miss Cleopatra Conolly**
P.O. Box 16
Grand Cayman KY1- 1801
CAYMAN ISLANDS

# Part One

## Recipes and Memories
## from
## Old East End

# Miss Cleo's Story

My name is Amareth Cleopatra Conolly, but everyone calls me Cleo. I have the honor of being Hospitality Ambassador at Morritt's Tortuga Club, the resort in East End, Grand Cayman, where I have worked since 1964. It was my first job outside of home and I was 39! I have stayed on even though the Club has changed owners several times, and I have become a very rich woman. Not rich in money, but in the many friends I have made from all over the world. Many of those friends were guests at the original Tortuga Club, which was built and owned by Americans Eric and Suzy Bergstrom in 1964. It was a small, 10 room family style resort (it grew to 14 rooms) that attracted guests from many countries. Many came back every year. I was the head chef and enjoyed my cooking. I stayed on in the kitchen at the Club every time it was sold. On September 4, 2004, Mr. David Morritt, the owner today, threw a big party to celebrate my 40th year at Tortuga Club. That was a week before Hurricane Ivan washed away my home and parts of the Club.

I was born in Colliers, East End, Grand Cayman on May 28, 1925, to James Hermon Conolly and Anna Louisa Watson Connolly, one of seven children. I grew up here in East End and have lived here all of my life—not even Hurricane Ivan could move me away!

I had one older sister, Olga Catherine, and five brothers, George Hubert, James Alvarez, Alfred Augustus, Harris Griffiths, and Frank Fernando Conolly, the youngest child. Frank and I are the only remaining children.

My great-great-grandfather, John Jarret Conolly, came to Grand Cayman from Ireland. He married a coloured woman from Bodden Town, but we don't know her history. So I can truly say that Miss Cleo is of Irish descent and that surprises quite a few people!

My family moved a few miles down the road to Sand Bluff in 1933, to my grandfather Zebulon Watson's daub and wattle house with wooden shingles, which was built in 1887. That house on the sea survived many storms and hurricanes, including the famous Hurricane of 1932 and Hurricane Gilbert in 1988, and it was my home until Hurricane Ivan destroyed it on September 12, 2004.

Life was very hard when we were young, and people in East End had very little. My father was away a lot. He worked as a cook for years on sailing ships traveling between Grand Cayman and Tampa, Cuba, Jamaica, Panama and the cays off Honduras and Nicaragua. He was an excellent cook! When he was home, he taught school for the local children who were too young to attend the Government School in East End. He also had a small grocery shop. But the most important things to him were his family and the Church. He was a lay pastor and taught Sunday School at the Gun Bay Presbyterian Church until he became too ill to do so. I was raised in a home with strong Christian values I have carried all of my life.

From the age of five I worked to help support the family, by making rope from Cayman thatch palm, which was an important product in Cayman and sold for export to Jamaica.

My family had it especially hard because my father took sick when he was 40 and I was only 5 years old. He came down with meningitis and had to stop working. For awhile, he couldn't' walk at all, and he suffered from seizures. My parents were away a lot after that, because they had to make the long trip to George Town by boat several times a month to see doctors and try to find treatment for my father.

We children had to learn to take care of most things ourselves after that. I had to help take care of the household with my brothers and sisters, as my father never worked again. In those days life was very hard because we had none of the luxuries East End has today.

There was no piped water in East End back then. We had to back water (carry in buckets using the back as a brace) and gather or chop wood to use in the caboose (wood burning stove). East End did not get piped water until 1995 and myself and many people today still have cisterns instead, buying water that is trucked in.

There was some electricity –but many houses didn't have it and ours was one that didn't. We take so much for granted today. We had so little when I was growing up compared to Cayman now. Looking back, I know things were very hard, but I didn't see it that way back then. We knew how to make the most of what we had and we were happy with that. Growing up in those days, especially with my parents having to be away so much, and my father being sick so young, taught us what was important. You don't need much to be happy if you have a good family. I don't think "rich" was a word we concerned ourselves with because we always had just what we needed.

From the time I was a little girl, I learned enough cookery from my mother to help feed our family and that was one of my chores. My father was a very good cook of course, and later, so were my brothers and sister Olga. I don't have those old recipes written down, they are only what I remember them to be. (See Old Time East End Cookery). The first thing I learned to make was "Rundown," with cornmeal dumplings, because we ate a lot of that. This was a simple one pot stew of fish or corned turtle or conch cooked in coconut milk with yam, cassava, bottler, plantain and other starches called ground provisions. East End people still enjoy it today, but it is time consuming to make.

When we were young, there was no school until you were age 7 and the school was a long walk from our home. Frank and I used to walk four miles each day to East End to school and then back again---sometimes all we carried for lunch was a piece of boiled cassava or bottler or roasted yam wrapped in foil.

When I was 7, the terrible Hurricane of 1932 devastated East End. Yes, my brother Frank and I survived that storm in my grandfather's house. The house stood up that 1932 storm and the tidal wave that washed over the land. I can still remember the awful noise and how terrified we were. But that house kept us safe and survived Hurricane Gilbert in 1988 too. That's where I lived from 1933 until Ivan destroyed it. So I have lived through the three worst hurricanes in the history of the Cayman Islands.

After I finished my education, which was about a sixth grade level, I stayed at home and dedicated myself to caring for my parents. My father died in 1960 at age 70. My mother lived longer, to age 83. She was a good woman and devoted to her family. Even though we were poor, my mother always made sure we dressed well and took care of ourselves. She used to call me a "fashion plate" because from a young age, I always loved clothes and enjoyed dressing for Sunday Church. My colorful dresses and my hats are things people came to expect and remember about Miss Cleo! They said I was always "dressed to the nines" when I left my house.

## A Job at Age 39 Becomes a Lifelong Career

Well, my mother always prayed that I would get a good job, with an American family –she never prayed I would get rich, only that I would find work. My mother's prayers were answered! I got that good job before she died at age 83, and that made her very happy. And it also made me rich too-- with many friends from all over the world who still write and call, including some from the USA who even call me their "Mom."

I took my first job at 39 outside the home in 1964 at the new Tortuga Club resort, the first hotel in East End, a 10 room resort built by Americans Eric and Suzy Bergstrom from Wisconsin which had just opened the year before.

When I went to interview for the job, I told Suzy I was not used to taking orders from anyone and that was going to be hard. She told me I would have to learn! Well, I tried and after two weeks as a server in the dining room, I was moved to the kitchen and learned a lot from Suzy about how to use kitchen appliances and cook foreign foods. She gave me my first cookbook, a thick Betty Crocker cookbook; after that, I enjoyed reading and discovering many new recipes and taught myself how to cook them. I eventually became head chef—the first female executive chef in the Cayman Islands. And that's where I worked for the next 35 years.

I taught Suzy some things too: about cooking our local fish, Cayman lobster and conch. I showed her about preparing breadfruit and ground provisions and coconuts and other Caymanian things that were new to her.

Now, another thing is that I have always loved to read. That helped me learn new ways of cooking and many new recipes. Suzy gave me my first cookbook in 1965, the *Betty Crocker Cookbook* and I kept that all these years until Ivan stole it. I started reading cookbooks and magazines that people gave me and looked for new recipes to try. And later when I traveled to see friends from the Club in the United States, I bought cookbooks from places I visited. I loved trying different foreign recipes my own way. I had a nice collection of cookbooks, but that was another thing that Ivan took away.

If I could name one thing that made a difference in the way Caymanians cooked and made life easier, it was the electric blender. I learned to use one when I first started working at Tortuga Club. This was a wonderful machine! It made making coconut milk so much easier! Now you still need to grate coconut on a box grater for some things, like coconut cream pie, but for everything else, the blender is most use. Coconut milk was so important to our cooking and making it took so much work and patience. That blender was a blessing!

One thing I had to learn from Suzy was how to cook with spirits. I don't drink spirits. I never had a drink in my life until my 40th birthday. I had my first and last drink of rum on that night! I got so sick I had to go to bed from that drink and I have never had a drink since! Some of the recipes Suzy taught me became favorites with the guests, like Lobster Thermidor and Crab Newburg. Those were very exotic dishes for that time in East End!

I planned the meals and did the ordering for the dinner menu and also cooked every day, but only dinners. I didn't do breakfast or lunches. We always had such wonderful fresh local seafood for guests. In those days, fishermen like Stanford Rankin would bring fresh fish for sale right to the kitchen door. These dishes and desserts like coconut cream and lime pies were my specialties and the ones guests loved most. We always had at least two fresh homemade desserts on the menu.

Now when I say menu, I don't mean a printed one. I didn't write one out. The girls would go around to each table and recite the dinner menu to guests. Sometimes that caused problems if they couldn't pronounce foreign dishes and I would have to come out and explain! We would serve each table individually and sometimes, each guest if it was a small table. It was very personal service and if there was enough left, seconds were always allowed. After dinner was finished, I would go around to each table to talk with guests, find out their likes and dislikes and they loved visiting with Chef Cleo.

My most famous guest was Prince Charles. I prepared a special lunch for his party, who visited the Club during the Royal Visit in 1967. I made my Prime Turtle Steak and he ate every bite and cleaned his plate! I was very proud of this!

I need to mention the other thing I have never been able to cook: barbeque and smoked foods. I had to let other cooks do at the Club do that for the guests. I am allergic to smoke, whether it is tobacco or from a grill or outdoor fire, and smoke is something I have to avoid or I will start coughing and can't stop. So that's why there is no chapter in my book about grilling and barbeque, or jerk. You won't find a charcoal grill in my yard.

I stayed on at Tortuga Club after the Bergstroms sold it in 1978 and tell people I was "sold along with the property" each time new owners took over—that was twice. The Club has grown much, much larger, from those 14 rooms to over 200 now. It is called Morritt's Tortuga Club and Morritts Grand Resort. It is nothing like what it was when I began as a dining room server so many years ago.

I finally retired from the kitchen in 2000 and took up a new position in the hotel lobby, as Hospitality Ambassador for Morritt's Tortuga Club. I enjoy greeting all the guests and talking with them, but I miss being able to cook for them. Some of my recipes, like my cornbread and bread pudding, are still on the menu. Guests who have been coming to the Club for years remember when I was the chef. Many of them, and people in Cayman, have asked me again and again for my recipes. That is why I have done this book.

Today at home again in my own kitchen, I still want certain things so I can cook properly: a good gas stove, a good heavy pot for making my beef and steaming yams, an electric blender and a pressure cooker. I don't care about all those other gadgets. You just can't make some things the right way without these.

And you still need patience and plain old "cooking sense" too. Even with a cookbook, you still have to have both of these in the kitchen.

# My Accomplishments and Awards

I am very proud of the awards I received for my work in tourism, including a special award from the Cayman Islands Hotel Association in 1983. In 1991 I was chosen as East End's first Tourism Industry Role Model during the Department of Tourism's first Tourism Awareness Week. The next year, Tortuga Club honored me with a plaque naming me the Tortuga Club Hospitality Ambassador. In 1996 I was honoured by the Queen with the Certificate and Badge of Honour for outstanding service to the community. During the 2003 Quincentennial Celebration, I was honored, along with my father, as one of the 500 Caymanians included on the Wall of Honour in Heroes Square in George Town.

Another important part of my life that I have to mention is that I have always been a strong Church woman and I am an Elder in the Gun Bay United Church in East End. I joined the choir when I was 15 and later taught Sunday School for more than 40 years. and I was the Sunday School superintendent for 27 years. I have held other positions at the Church and have been a member of the Church Women's Guild and Girl's Brigade. I was honored for my years of dedicated service. Being a strong Church woman and my faith in God has helped me overcome life's trials and tribulations. People have said that I am a strong woman and a brave one too and I have God to thank for making me so, especially during recent years.

On May 23, 2003, I found a lump in my right breast, but I put off going to the doctor because it was my birthday week and I always celebrate my birthday. In June they found out I had breast cancer and had surgery, a mastectomy that kept me in the George Town Hospital for 15 days. I am still being treated with medication, but that is the way with breast cancer. I thank God for letting me be a cancer survivor today.

The next big trial came in September 2004. This was supposed to be a happy month for me! On September 3, Mr. David Morritt threw a big party in honor of my 40 years of service to Morritt's Tortuga Club, with over 100 invited guests! The next day, I left Grand Cayman to fly to Boston to visit friends---it was my first vacation in many years.

But a week later, I was sitting in Boston, worrying about my family and my house in East End as Hurricane Ivan was heading right at the island. I was able to get through to my brother Frank by cell phone and heard the bad news: that the storm had devastated Grand Cayman, the sea came through his house---and my house was gone. I changed my plans the next day to fly home—friends told me not to go back because it was so bad, but I couldn't stay away. The drive from the airport to Sand Bluff was one of the biggest shocks of my life as we passed through so much destruction. I was seven when I lived through the famous Hurricane of 1932, and my house survived that storm and the horrible hurricane of 1988 before that. But not this one. I lost my house and all of my possessions, including my awards and photographs, and had to move in with family for the first time in my adult life.

The year after Ivan was very hard, but not just because I had lost my home. I had no job to go to, and after 40 years, that was very hard for me because I love to work and love my job. I am grateful that Mr. Morritt agreed to give me a small salary every month so I could have my health insurance. But I missed seeing people and missed my work as Hospitality Ambassador.

Thanks to the kindness of the Bergstrom children and the Friends of Miss Cleo, I have a new house in the same place where my family home stood. God bless them! I am happy to say, Frank and I are both back in our own homes and I am back at my job today. I don't want to retire yet and every day brings new gifts. The richest of all are the friends I have made who have been so good to me.

I should tell you that I have decided not to travel during September ever again. It seems that every time I have gone on vacation in September, a bad hurricane hits Cayman. In 1988, I was in Houston, Texas visiting friends and Hurricane Gilbert, another bad storm, mashed up Cayman. So I want to reassure everyone, Cleo is staying home in September from now on!

## My Brother Frank

I want to mention my brother Frank before I close because he has been an important part of my life and made many contributions to Cayman tourism too. Frank is my only living brother as well as my next door neighbor with his wife in Sand Bluff, and his son McFarlane, who is a Vice President at Cayman National Bank and family live just down from him.

When Frank was 25 he went to sea. He learned a lot about the world because he traveled all over with National Bulk Carriers for 14 years. He was a very good boatswain, overseeing the maintenance of those big ships. Frank returned home to East End in 1967 to raise a family and began to work in the tourism industry, as bartender at the Tortuga Club. He can tell you stories about that! Frank won awards for several of his drink recipes too. Later, he worked his way up to general manager.

Frank left East End for awhile in 1982, to work as Resident and Assistant Manager at the Royal Palms Hotel on Seven Mile Beach. (The hotel burned down in 1988 and the Reef Grill Restaurant and beach bar is on that site now.) He returned to Tortuga Club in 1984 again as General Manager and stayed there until 1992. Frank was a director in the Cayman Islands Hotel Association for many years as well and was honored by the Queen in 2004 with a Certificate and Badge of Honour for his contributions to tourism and the community. Today he has his own business and drives a taxi between the airport and East End.

Frank was and still is a strong Church man and is an Elder at the United Church of Jamaican and Cayman at Gun Bay. And some people do not know this, but my brother Frank is a good cook too! He makes the best cakes, which is something I never liked to do. Many people say his heavy cakes are the best in Cayman.

Frank and his wife and family suffered badly after Ivan too. His house, which is next to mine, was damaged and had to be almost rebuilt. But Frank is as strong as I am, and he is now back to driving his taxi van, taking visitors to and fro, all around Grand Cayman. God has been good to us and we are grateful every day for that.

**God Bless you all,**
Cleopatra Conolly

I wrote this for my niece Ann for her bridal shower years ago, and wanted to share it with my friends. It is worth remembering today, especially young people who expect everything to happen at once.

### "Patience: Recipe for a Happy Marriage"

**2 cups of your husband's love**
**1 cup of yours**
**½ cup of Meekness**
**¼ cup of Goodness**
**3 teaspoons full of Peace**
**1 teaspoon of Faith**

Mix all ingredients together well, then sprinkle on top a generous amount of Patience and you will have a happy marriage.

# Speech By
## Miss Cleopatra Connolly,
### East End's First Tourism Industry Role Model Award

# Tourism Awareness Week October 1991

*In September 1991 during the Cayman Islands Department of Tourism's first Tourism Awareness Week, Miss Cleo Conolly was honored as East End's Tourism Industry Role Model for her outstanding contribution to the industry. The following was transcribed from Cleo's handwritten speech when accepting her award and commemorative plaque. In it, she shared personal information about her 27 years in Cayman's tourism industry.*

During a public meeting in East End in 1975, Hon. Warren Connolly, MLA from East End, congratulated Mrs. Suzy Bergstrom for the reputation the Tortuga Club had built up in the tourism field since it opened in 1963. At that meeting Suzy praised her staff for our fine service and pride in our work during the past 11 years.

At that meeting, I received an Honorary Turtle Award from Suzy for my famous foods as the first local and only female chef at the time.

In 1977 I took a course in Customer Contact. I used to cook dinner every night, and then I would go into the dining room and visit all the guests in person. This was something I did naturally, as part of my personality.

In 1978 Susie and Eric sold the Club and I was "sold" along with it.

In 1979 I sent a recipe (for Cleo's Conch Stew) to the Caribbean Kitchen Salon culinary competition in Ocho Rios, Jamaica. I received a Certificate of Accomplishment award for that recipe. It helped make up the first Caribbean cookbook that was printed by the Caribbean Hotel Association in Puerto Rico.

In 1980 I took another training course in the Community College in Newlands. Later that year, I took part in the Pirates Week cooking competition, which was held at the Holiday Inn. I was awarded a plaque for Third Place for my Prime Turtle Steak recipe.

In 1983 I was awarded the Annual Tourism Award by the Cayman Islands Hotel Association in recognition of my sincere contribution to tourism in the Cayman Islands. Since then I have been "sold" twice when Tortuga Club changed owners.

The tourism industry is something I am proud of and I am glad that I can be a part of it. I must say it has been a Godsend to Grand Cayman.

Some time last year I met a couple from the cruise ship when I was in town. They asked me where to find a certain place and we started talking. They said "Why doesn't the Government station you at the tourist landing to meet people! We have so enjoyed talking with a real Caymanian!"

I am always glad to help people because I have gained a lot of friends abroad by working in the tourism industry. This September 4 (1991) was 27 years since I've been at the Tortuga Club. During these 27 years I have had some good times and some bad times, but the good times are what I remember of these many years.

In the tourism industry, one thing you have to bear in mind: we are here to please the tourist. It doesn't matter how wrong a tourist is, they are always right. And it only takes one or two unhappy ones and they can make it bad for us. I was head chef and supervisor of the dining room and I worked for 10 hours a day. After dinner was served, I used to go into the dining room and visit every table to find out from my guests their likes and dislikes. I am happy to say I made a lot of guests happy.

Some may say "why wouldn't you go to work in town? You could make more money", but I felt that if I could be of service, let it be here in my own district of East End.

I will close with something I want to share, about what has guided me all these years. It was written many years ago by my first cousin Fulbert Conolly, who passed away, and it has stuck with me all my life:

*Whatever you are doing, let your standard be high.*
*That the goal makes no difference is surely a lie*
*You'll never hit higher than the spot of your aim*
*In soul, mind and body, you'll find it the same.*
*Don't say you can't reach it and then cease to try-*
*Do your best every moment and always aim high!*

# Roast Yams and Coconut Rice:

## Memories of My East End Girlhood

Many guests at the Club have asked me over the years, "Miss Cleo, where did you learn to cook?"

Well I guess you could say that cooking is just like common sense to me and is in my blood. My mother and father were both good cooks. Later in life, my brothers James and Harris, like my father, were cooks onboard ships and my sister Olga was also a very good cook. But I learned to cook from my mother, who taught me to "make do with what was on hand." By the time I was five, I knew how to help prepare meals for the family, which I had to do very often. Back then, you didn't "eat out" unless it was at a special Church function where everyone brought something!

When I was growing up, East End was very different from the way it is today. We were very poor and things were hard for us, especially with my father being sick at such an early age. My parents had to be away from home very often so he could be treated in George Town. But we made do with what we had on hand, and we were happy.

We cooked our meals in the kitchen. Some called it the cook room but we called it the kitchen. It was a little wooden covered area or small building apart from the house. It had a caboose, a wooden box filled with sand, and that's what we cooked with. You couldn't risk the fire too close to the house. We didn't have a stove or an oven, of course back then. My mother cooked in iron pots over wood fire. You had two iron bars over the fire to put the pot on. We used wood that we children gathered: grape tree, mahogany wood, plop nut—anything that was dry. That was one of our daily chores.

We ate very simply, but those simple meals took a lot of work. And I remember those meals being so delicious! Today you hear foreign chefs talking about cooking "slow food" like it's something new. Well, Caymanians know what slow food is because that was how we made our traditional dishes! We had so little to cook with that we made good use of every part of every thing and most food was cooked so slowly. We were rich though. Our food was fresh and healthy.

We would wrap ripe breadfruit in foil, or yam and sweet potatoes and roast them in the ashes of the fire---we didn't have any breadfruit trees in East End years ago, so breadfruit was a special treat that came from George Town. That might be our lunch to take to school. There was no junk food in those days!

The first dish I learned to make was "Rundown" with cornmeal dumplings. This was a simple one pot stew of fish or corned turtle or conch cooked in coconut milk with yam, cassava, bottler, plantain and other starches called ground provisions. Now we had few seasonings! Coconut milk, limes, salt and black pepper was what we used for flavor, and some people liked a little country pepper too. There were no onions or garlic, and not many scallions, or things like ketchup and Worcestershire sauce to cook with. Things we take for granted today: tinned beef, flour, sugar, rice, beans, onions and especially fresh dairy products, were luxuries to us. There were no convenience foods—it was a miracle to us when boxed macaroni and cheese and tinned evaporated milk came to the shelves.

We had plenty of coconuts. When I was little, we made coconut milk the old way. We used a piece of the brown coconut mesh from the tree (called the coir) or a dried sea fan that had washed up on the beach. That was our sieve. And we used a box grater to hand grate the coconut meat. But coconut milk was one of the most important ingredients in the kitchen, and no matter how much work it took, we had to have it.

There was always fresh fish, whelks, lobster, conch, and turtle—and turtle eggs. We steamed fish or cooked it in coconut milk for rundown, or fried it in coconut oil or Crisco and that was delicious hot or cold.

Scale fish like grouper and small snapper were favorites for rundown. For steam fish, we especially liked ocean turbot and old wives, which people today call triggerfish now. Sometimes we also ate what we called "shellfish" (Cowfish or trunkfish) which was strange little fish you sometimes found hiding in turtle grass when looking for conches. We would chase it up into the shallows and catch it. You had to peel (skin) it first, then chop up the flesh and season it, and bake it on a seagrape leaf. That was delicious too!

One bad thing about fish was getting poisoned, and most often it was barracuda. Even though people know about this today, many still eat it. If you got poisoned (ciguatera, a serious kind of fish poisoning) you would be sick for months and after that, all kinds of seafood tasted bad, like gall and you would have tingly feelings in your arms and legs, and sometimes the face too. It was like palsy. I got poisoned when I was younger and some say that that's why I can't eat lobster and some things today.

I have never liked crab either, not sea crabs (East End actually has stone crabs) or the blue land crabs. I didn't like to chase them and was never good at pickin' them and pickin' crab is a job in itself. Once in awhile my family ate stew crab in coconut milk but we were not big crab eaters. Some local people have trouble with crab because they are allergic to it.

Turtle has always been a traditional dish in Cayman, especially in East End. Here, years ago, many men went to sea for months as turtle fishermen, far away to Honduras, Nicaragua and Cuba. My family ate turtle like most people in East End, usually as stew. True Caymanian turtle stew is a very simple dish and has few if any spices—just a mix of turtle meats and pieces of bone and fin, and salt and pepper and maybe a little country pepper, cooked over low heat for a long time so the turtle meat gives up its oil. We would also make corned turtle to preserve it to use in rundown later. Many believed that turtle also had certain medicinal use. One doctor told my mother to eat turtle fin to calm her gallbladder. But when I got older, I couldn't' eat turtle. It made me feel weak and dizzy. Doctors never could figure out why that was.

My mother and father had one rule: we never ate scale fish on Sundays. That was my family's way. We would have shellfish, like conch or lobster or whelk, or sometimes a chicken. Like everyone else back then, we always had chickens in the yard. And we didn't have meat except at Christmas. We raised pigs and cows but not goats. We never killed an animal other than chickens during the year, only at Christmas.

We grew plenty of ground provisions like yam, coco and bottlers, plantains and such good tasting pumpkins! They were bright orange and have such a rich taste. There were plenty of limes, and June plums, guineps, guava, melons and wild mangos. We grew barley and corn that is called guinea corn today, that we roasted, or hung and dried, and grated for porridge or cakes. What people eat as corn grits today it something we threw to the chickens—and I like grits now, but we didn't know about cooking them back then.

Back then we didn't have breadfruit and pear (avocado) in East End. A nice ripe breadfruit or pear was a special treat from far away in George Town. And oh, there is nothing better than a ripe pear that spreads like butter on a piece of bread! That is a meal in itself and still a Caymanian favorite today. We didn't have salads or greens, except sometimes a bunch of callaloo from a lady down in Gun Bay. But we stayed healthy. My mother knew about many herbs and plants, especially the aloe plant, that were used as remedies for everything from stomach ache and fever to coughs and even arthritis.

Yam is still one of my favorite foods and you know, our yams are very healthy foods, especially for women. I especially like the white yam from Cayman Brac, which is hard to get today. When I was a little girl, a piece of boiled or roast yam wrapped in foil was a whole meal. We carried this to school as lunch. Things we take for granted today, like flour, sugar and rice, were expensive luxuries.

We had bottlers, which are delicious: they are like a stubby plantain, but much sweeter and starchier. My mother would make porridge or cakes from grated bottler. We had a lot of fruits: small sweet bananas, papaya, melons, guava, and wild mango and of course coconut. And we sometimes had wonderful yellow fleshed breadfruit you can't find often today, and ripe pears from George Town. Tinned cream (evaporated milk), rice, flour and sugar –the coarse brown or wet sugar from Jamaica--were all luxuries.

We didn't eat many baked sweets—we ate fruits like guava for our sugar and sweet treats. For birthdays or special occasions, and Church functions, there would be a pot cake. This was like a steamed pudding, not as rich as a heavy cake, and the best ones were made from bottlers.

Years later, I learned to enjoy dishes that are called "local" food now, but many of these are really Jamaican or Honduran, and not Caymanian. I love things like rice and beans and cowfoot. Even though it's gluey, I like the taste and the texture of it! Now these dishes are from modern times, because they are made with ingredients that were scarce in East End 60 years ago. I find fewer and fewer people know how to cook them too. In today's busy world, most would rather buy take away or eat out.

# The Amazing Coconut:
## A Caymanian Staple

What would Caymanians have done without the coconut? It has fed and cured us for centuries. It is the main ingredient and base for many of our traditional recipes. The humble coconut is every Caribbean cook's godsend. It has inspired hundreds of recipes, from sweet snacks like coconut drops and gizzadas to seafood stews and desserts. It is the most versatile cooking ingredient we have.

Coconut water right from the nut is a legendary folk remedy. Coconut water keeps the kidneys clean and helps cure infections. There is nothing better. I had a whole yard full of coconut trees before Hurricane Ivan and that's the one thing I miss today.

Fresh coconut is nothing like the bagged sweetened coconut in stores today, which also has its purpose in baking. The oil in fresh coconut improves many recipes and gives them a rich, nutty coconut flavor. The same goes for coconut milk. The canned products sold today are a convenience but they lack the coconut oil that gives fresh coconut milk its rich flavor and makes it a favorite Caymanian cooking ingredient.

Today many Western nutritionists have finally admitted what Asian cultures have known for thousands of years ago: that coconut, especially virgin coconut oil, is a very healthy natural food.

# Coconut Milk

*Today we have canned coconut milk in every grocery store, but the best kind is still home made. In days gone, I used a box grater and grated each coconut by hand, but today I use a blender. I cut up the meat into small pieces and put it in a blender and add the hot water, and blend to a fine mash (puree). Then I strain it to make my coconut milk. If you must get 3 cups of coconut milk out of one coconut, it won't be nearly as rich as if you blend with a smaller amount of water.*

### INGREDIENTS:
**1 medium dry coconut, meat removed**
**1-3/4 cups hot water**

### DIRECTIONS:
Peel the brown skin from the coconut meat. Grate the meat of one medium coconut into a large bowl—this will be about 3 cups. Add about 1-3/4 cups very hot water. Stir the mixture to blend and allow to cool. Strain the liquid through cheesecloth or a fine sieve and squeeze to extract as much juice as possible. Discard the trash or as we do, throw it out for the chickens. Store in refrigerator if not using right away. This will give you about a cup and a half of rich coconut milk.

### Coconut facts:
- 1 medium dry brown coconut weighs about 1-1/2 lbs. and yields about ½ cup coconut water and 3-4 cups grated meat. This will make about 1 -1/2 cups rich coconut milk.
- To get the most coconut water, choose a young green coconut which will also give you the delicious coconut "jelly" which is the meat before it hardens.
- Fresh coconut water should be refrigerated and used within 24 hours or frozen.
- **Coconut Milk is not Coconut Water, the liquid straight from the nut**. Coconut water is one of nature's purest ingredients. Coconut milk has to be made.
- In Cayman, there are about 8 varieties of coconut and the quality of the nut can vary tremendously. So can the yield of meat---which depends on the age of the nut. A young green nut will give you jelly instead of firm meat.
- Be sure you pick a fresh coconut. Shake it—it should be full of "water." The fresher the coconut, the more water it has.
- Even dry brown coconuts have a freshness limit. Ones older than four months are likely to be too old to use.
- To substitute fresh grated or finely chopped coconut for processed shredded or flaked coconut, use 1 cup fresh grated to 1-1/3 cup firmly packed shredded or flaked.
- To toast coconut, spread in a single layer on a baking sheet and bake at 325 degrees for 8-10 minutes, until just light golden brown.
- Coconut meat is sensitive to high heat. Add at the last minute to sauces or sprinkle over dishes, like curry.
- Fresh grated or finely chopped coconut meat can be covered with milk and soaked for 6 hours in refrigerator, then drained. This will give it similar moisture content as the commercial shredded or flaked coconut.

# Coconut Water

If you have nothing else but coconut water, you won't starve to death. The nutrients it contains will prevent malnourishment. Fresh coconut water contains many essential minerals such as potassium and, calcium. The water of immature (green) coconuts is the most nutritious natural liquid on earth. It is better than Gatorade and other sports drinks for fighting dehydration and preventing heat stroke in the tropical heat. Older Caymanians know that it helps cool the body, aids in digestion and cleans the kidneys and urinary tract. And overall, it's a wonderful restorative tonic for the elderly and sick.

# Old Time East End Cookery & Recipes

It is important that you know the difference between coconut water, and coconut milk. Coconut water is the pure liquid that comes right from the nut. It is best when it comes from a green or half hard coconut, not a dry brown one. Coconut milk is what you make from the grated meat of a dry brown coconut which is combined with water and then strained. If you want to make rich coconut milk, you would use less water. And coconut trash is the strained coconut meat left behind, which we feed to the chickens in the yard.

# Coconut Rice

*Rice was a luxury for my family and a real treat, especially the way my mother made it. She would cook it in a heavy pot, with coconut water and coconut milk over a very low flame until the rice was very soft, and then pour the mixture into a pan and let it set until firm-almost like a rice cake. To serve, she would slice pieces for all us children-was that delicious! Here is a recipe you can try:*

### INGREDIENTS:

2 cups rice (long grain, not parboiled or short)
Water
2-1/2 cups coconut water
1 teaspoon salt
2 cups coconut milk** (1-1/2 cups for drier rice)

### DIRECTIONS:

Wash the rice in strainer under cool water. Drain well, place rice in heavy pot and add coconut water and salt. Stir several times. Bring to a boil, then add coconut milk and stir well. Reduce heat to a low flame, cover and cook undisturbed for 15 minutes, then uncover and check rice to make sure it isn't too dry. Add a little more coconut milk if necessary and cook until rice is very soft and liquid is absorbed. Remove from heat and spoon into a lightly buttered 2 – quart baking dish or pan and let rest, covered, or chill until firm. You can then slice the rice and serve it the old fashioned way.

*\*\* (If you want your rice dry and fluffy, continue cooking until rice has absorbed all liquid, then remove from heat, cover and let steam for 10 minutes.)*

# Cayman Heavy Cornmeal Dumplings

*These were as important to many dishes like rundown as the fish or meat itself! Men especially would try to dip into the pot first and get those dumplings!*

### INGREDIENTS:

2 cups corn meal
1-1/2 cups hot water
1-1/2 cups flour
1/4 teaspoon salt
2 tablespoons sugar

### DIRECTIONS:

In a large bowl, mix the cornmeal and water together until blended—this step is important so the dumplings won't be tough. Then use a wooden spoon to mix in the remaining ingredients until blended. Wet your fingers and pinch off pieces of dough and pat out to flatten using your hands. Lay on top of your rundown or stew and cover. Cook 20 minutes.

# Cayman Johnnycake

*What we called Johnnycake in old times was nothing like what you find today. It was very simple dough made from flour, salt, baking powder and water. We had no shortening, oil, butter or sugar. You would add just enough water to be able to knead it and shape it into a round loaf. Then you would "bake" it, by putting it right in the ashes of the fire. I don't know how the old people did this, without all the ashes sticking to the johnnycake. Others baked it on the caboose, or in a hole in the ground, with coals on the bottom and on top the old way, in a cast iron pan so it formed a delicious crust all over. This is a "modern" recipe made with a little sugar and shortening, which makes a richer Johnnycake.*

**INGREDIENTS:**
2-1/2 cups flour
1 tablespoon baking powder
¼ teaspoon salt
2 teaspoons sugar
1/3 cup lard or Crisco solid shortening
2/3 cup water or enough to make soft dough

**DIRECTIONS:**
Mix together dry ingredients. Cut in lard or shortening, or rub in with fingertips. Add water slowly, just enough to make a soft dough. Knead a few times until dough is smooth and holds together. Let rest for 10 minutes. Shape into a 8-9 inch round loaf and put into a greased hot skillet. Flatten slightly if necessary to fit, and cover pan. Cook at medium- high heat over stove, turning, until brown on both sides. Reduce heat and cover, continue cooking 15 to 20 minutes.

# Fritters (Flitters)

*These little fried dough pieces are what many Caymanians eat with fried fish and are favorites at breakfast. Jamaicans call them Johnnycakes, but Caymanian Johnnycake is very different as I have already mentioned.*

### INGREDIENTS:
2 cups flour
1 tablespoon baking powder
½ teaspoon salt
1 teaspoon sugar
2 tablespoons Crisco solid shortening
About 1/2 cup water

### DIRECTIONS:
Sift the flour, baking powder, salt and sugar into a medium mixing bowl. Using a pastry blender or your fingers cut or rub in the Crisco until the mixture resembles fine crumbs. Add enough water, a little at a time, to form a soft dough. Turn the dough onto a lightly floured surface and flour your hands. Knead the dough until smooth, adding a little more flour if necessary to work easily. Pinch off pieces of dough (about 2 tablespoons each) and roll into 2-inch balls, and then flatten into ½ inch thick circles. Heat enough vegetable oil to cover cakes completely in a large heavy skillet until hot (375 F). Fry cakes until golden on each side, and then remove and drain on paper towels. This makes 12 cakes. Serve warm.

# Salads & Vegetables

We didn't have lettuce or fancy greens back when I was growing up. A head of cabbage was a rare luxury to us. I didn't know about such things as salad until I was working in the kitchen at the Club.

Our vegetables were ground provisions we grew in our yard and sometimes, a breadfruit or pear from George Town. Now we did have callaloo once in awhile. I think Miss Julie down the road in Gun Bay used to grow that in her yard. I remember something like that from when I was a girl.

In Cayman, the nearest thing to a salad we had back in the 1960s and early 1970s would have been chopped cabbage, plain or with a little dressing, with shredded carrots and maybe a few scallions.

In East End, people made breadfruit salad with canned mixed vegetables and maybe a little beet but not hard boiled eggs. We still like breadfruit salad today. Remember, back then, things like vegetable oil, mayonnaise and salad dressings—even tinned vegetables, were luxuries to us.

# "Salad" or traditional Cole Slaw

*A cabbage was a real treat for us 50 years ago but today, people take something like this for granted. Many use mayonnaise instead of oil and vinegar. You can use more or less dressing to suit your taste.*

## INGREDIENTS:
6 cups shredded green cabbage
1 cup shredded carrots
½ cup chopped onion or scallions
½ cup chopped seeded green sweet pepper
1/2 cup vegetable oil
1/3 cup white vinegar or lime juice
1-2 tablespoons sugar, or to taste, if desired
1 teaspoon ground black pepper
Salt to taste

## DIRECTIONS:
In large bowl, combine the cabbage, carrots, onion and green pepper and mix well. Combine the oil, vinegar, sugar if desired, salt and pepper. Mix until sugar is dissolved and pour over cabbage mixture. Toss lightly and chill for at least an hour.

*(Today, some nice additions to this might be: ½ teaspoon celery seeds and 1 teaspoon Coleman's mustard; ½ cup chopped sweet red pepper or 2 tablespoons sliced ripe olives).*

# Crab Cayman Style

I know there are crabs in the sea here in East End, both shallow and very deep. I have seen those hard orange ones called stone crabs too, but we never ate them. My family sometimes ate the big blue land crabs but they weren't a favorite thing. After the spring rains, we children would go out at night and catch those crabs. They had to be cleaned before we would eat them. We didn't eat stuffed crab backs. We ate stew crab. We picked out the meat from the backs and the fingers and that was work! Then we cooked it with coconut milk, like rundown. It wasn't until later that people started to make stuffed crab backs. We never had enough leftover bread and the kind of seasonings available today.

I don't like land crab. I know what they eat. Oh I know they are supposed to be fed mangos and fruits to clean out their insides before eating, but even after that, I don't like them. Besides, when I tried to pick the crab, too much shell ended up in the crab. And you can't have that. Some people are good at picking crabs, but not me. It's a lot of work to clean enough crabs to make a meal.

I did serve crab backs at the Club a few times, but not often. It wasn't the kind of thing you could serve most visitors without explaining what it was, and that made it sound worse. And it looked bad on the plate. No matter how hard you try, you can't make a crab back look attractive for a tourist. They have to want to eat it. When I made crab dishes for dinner at the Club, I used imported crab meat that came in a tin to make Crab Newburg, which guests loved.

# Baked Crab (Crab Back)

*People today use a lot more spices, but in the old days, there was no Worcestershire sauce or Old Bay seasoning and so this was a very simple recipe. During the rainy season when the crabs came out at night, chasing and catching crabs was fun for the children. Not me! I let my brothers do that. You had to keep the crabs in a pen and feed them fruit scraps for several days to clean them (purge) or they would taste foul.*

### INGREDIENTS:
6 live blue land crabs
1 large onion, chopped
3 scallions, chopped fine
1 large green sweet pepper, seeded and chopped fine
¼ cup margarine
1 teaspoon salt (some like seasoning salt)
½ teaspoon black pepper
Few slivers country pepper, seeded, if desired
Juice of one lime
1- 2 cups dried breadcrumbs

### INGREDIENTS:
Make sure the crabs have been purged and are clean. In a large heavy pot, boil the crabs, a few at a time, for 20 minutes. Be careful to avoid the biters (claws) and watch that the crabs don't jump up out of the pot at you! Remove the cooked crabs and let cool until you can handle them. Pick out the meat from shell (claws and body and legs, if big enough) and throw away the gall. Pick over carefully to remove any pieces of shell or grit. Flake the crab meat and set aside. Scrub the empty shells (body) well and pat dry.

Preheat oven to 350. In a large skillet, melt the margarine and cook the vegetables until soft. Stir in crabmeat, salt and pepper (and hot pepper if desired), lime juice and enough breadcrumbs to make a soft filling—not too much or it will be too dry. Spoon into crab shells and bake on greased baking sheet for 30 minutes, until lightly browned.

# Fish "Cayman style"

This recipe has gotten very confused in the last 50 years. If you want my opinion, true old time Cayman style fish is a very simple dish. You wash the fish in lime juice or vinegar and water first, then season with salt and pepper and steam it, usually with onion and sweet green pepper. Pan frying is also good (meaning sautéed, not deep fried) in coconut oil. Many people think leftover fish cooked in coconut oil is even better cold!

We used only a few seasonings: salt, black pepper, scallions, sweet peppers, thyme ---and coconut. Coconut milk and coconut oil were as much a seasoning as anything else and gave everything a wonderful flavor. Some also liked to use a little hot pepper—which could be mutton peppers or Scotch bonnets. Mutton peppers are milder, obling peppers and are not as common today.

Today "Fish Cayman style" in a restaurant often means fish overcooked in a thick tomato sauce heavily seasoned with hot pepper and other spices. Tomatoes and tomato sauces are not traditional Caymanian ingredients and fish done this way is not a true Caymanian recipe.

Steaming: When we say "steam" a fish, we mean put in a pan with a little coconut oil or Crisco and cook, covered, over low heat with diced onion, sweet pepper and hot pepper, if desired. The vegetables and fish will give up their liquids and this will let the fish steam and make a delicious flavor.

# Caymanian names for fish:

- Ocean Turbot is a deep water ocean triggerfish and old wife is a Queen triggerfish—both are real Caymanian favorites

- Boxfish or "shellfish" is a cowfish or trunkfish---it bakes up whole like a cake when done

- Silks are red snappers

- Grouper can be different kinds of grouper and those little fish some call hinds.

- Queen fish is a wahoo

- Tuna means yellowfin tuna. We seldom bother with others except as bait

- Dolphin is the beautiful green & yellow fish, or "dolphin fish" not the mammal. Only recently have Caymanians called dolphin "mahi-mahi," the Hawaiian name" to distinguish it from the mammal for tourists.

- Kingfish is a Spanish mackerel---not common in these waters

- Snapper means hogfish, mutton snapper, yellowtail snappers

- Ocean yellowtail is a rainbow runner

- Prop Props are black durgons

- Whelks are West Indian top shells

- Sea cats are octopus

- Conch is a Queen conch, not any other kind of mollusk

- "Sea beef" is a chiton, a small shellfish that grows on the ironshore, These are protected now, but not something most Caymanians would eat anyway.

# Ocean Turbot

I would be so pleased if someone would bring me a cleaned turbot or old wife (Queen triggerfish) to cook today, but like so many things, they are hard to come by. I don't think many people know how to clean them and it probably sounds like too much work. But, oh are they delicious and sweet!

After you clean the turbot, you have to remove the skin (some used a pair of pliers to do this. It comes off in a few strips), wash the fish in cold water with a little lime juice to freshen. Then just leave the fish whole to steam.

**Hashed:** The old folks say they liked their turbot hashed, or minced. You clean and season the fish the same way, then cut into chunks and cook in a small amount of water until the meat falls away easily from the bones. Drain the fish, remove the bones and mash it. Heat 2 tablespoons coconut oil or Crisco with 1 cup chopped onions, 1 cup chopped sweet green pepper and mutton pepper or other hot pepper as desired, and cook until vegetables are soft. Add the minced fish to the vegetables and cook until heated through over low heat, turning with a spoon so it doesn't scorch on the bottom. Season with salt and pepper to taste.

# Queen fish (Wahoo)

This is another favorite East End fish, but it is mostly available in winter and spring. You can catch small ones year round, but the big ones start coming in November. I have seen these fish as big as 100 pounds and more! Some people like filets, but most usually cook this fish as steaks-steamed or pan-fried. You should not cut wahoo steaks or filets too thin and be careful not to overcook it, because it is a dry fish. You should remove the "V" bloodline, the dark meat at the top of the steak, and the skin too, if using filets, so the fish doesn't taste foul.

# Stuffed Wahoo

*This is my original recipe which I have never seen duplicated in Cayman! It's a different way of using the flavors of steam fish and surprises people whenever you serve it.*

### INGREDIENTS:
8 Wahoo steaks or skinless filets, about 1/2 inch thick
Lime juice
Salt and black pepper
Butter or oil

Stuffing:
¼ cup vegetable or olive oil
1 cup chopped onion
1 cup chopped celery
1 cup chopped sweet green pepper

### DIRECTIONS:
Preheat oven to 350 F. Line a 9 x 13-inch baking dish or pan with foil and lightly oil or butter. Wash the wahoo pieces with cold water and lime juice and pat dry. Arrange 4 pieces of fish in a single layer in the pan. Sprinkle with salt and black pepper.

In a medium skillet, heat the oil and sauté the vegetables, stirring frequently, until soft. Divide the stuffing evenly among the four pieces and spread over each. Place remaining pieces on top and brush generously with oil, then sprinkle with salt and pepper and paprika if desired. Bake lightly covered with foil for 25 minutes until fish just begins to flake easily and is done.

# Cowfoot

*I am including this old recipe because I like cowfoot. Some of our local dishes have strange names we have forgotten the origin of. Others are what they are, and this is one of them. I read that gelatin is made from cow's hooves, and that is the reason for the gluey texture of this dish. This is one of my favorite meals because I like that "gluey-ness." Some people like more seasoning and add minced garlic or hot pepper with the scallion. This can be made in a pressure cooker, which cuts the cooking time.*

**INGREDIENTS:**
4 pounds cowfoot, cut into 2-3 inch pieces
4 quarts water
2 teaspoons salt
3 large stalks scallion
1 large sprig thyme
black pepper and salt to taste
Broad beans or provisions or vegetables of choice
(Irish potato, yam, sweet potato, carrots)

**DIRECTIONS:**
In a large pot or Dutch oven, combine the cowfoot, water and salt and bring to a boil. Reduce heat to medium, cover and cook for an hour, or until the meat is soft. Drain the cowfoot, reserving 4 cups of the cooking liquid. Let the liquid cool 15 minutes and skim off any fat that rises. (You can use the remaining liquid to make sweetened jelly, an old time treat.)

In large saucepan, combine the cowfoot (meat removed from bones if you want), reserved 4 cups liquid, seasonings and 2 cups cut up vegetables of choice. Bring to a boil, then reduce to medium low and simmer 30 minutes or until vegetables are tender. Some like to let this cool to room temperature before eating, so the mixture is more like jelly. Makes 4 servings.

# Cornmeal Custard

*I remember my mother and sister making this from homemade cornmeal, which was made by grating dry corn we grew ourselves. I never had the exact recipe, since she didn't write anything down in those days! Some call it custard top cornbread. It is eaten cold as dessert, not warm as a bread or side dish. There are many different recipes for it and everyone has an opinion.*

*The secret is to use homemade coconut milk, which has more coconut oil than canned milk. And my opinion is to always use more flour than cornmeal, or the custard won't rise properly. Some people use eggs, but old recipes did not, because eggs were very dear. And the vanilla is a modern addition; that was not something we had often. The brown sugar used was the "wet" coarse brown sugar from Jamaica, which was all we had years ago. You can still find it today in Cayman supermarkets."*

### INGREDIENTS:
2 cups all purpose flour
1 cup yellow cornmeal
3 cups brown sugar
1/2 teaspoon salt
8 cups freshly made coconut milk
1 tablespoon vanilla
¼ cup butter or margarine, melted

### DIRECTIONS:
Preheat oven to 350 F. Lightly grease or spray with PAM a large (10 x 17") baking dish. Combine flour, cornmeal, sugar and salt in a large mixing bowl and stir well with fork or wire whisk to blend. Slowly stir coconut milk, stirring until mixture is smooth-there must be no lumps. Add vanilla and blend well. Pour batter into prepared pan and swirl in the melted butter with a spatula or knife, mixing well.

Bake at 350 for 1-1/2 hours or until top is golden brown and custard on top is set. This will become firmer as it cools. Remove pan from oven and allow cooling on wire rack for 30 minutes, then refrigerate until cold.

# Old Time Steamed Pudding (Duff)

*This was a special dessert treat usually saved for Christmas or other holidays. Most people don't know how to steam a pudding today, so I have put those instructions below after the recipe. Now, some of us older Caymanians remember a thing called Duff, and this was very similar, only made with stew guava or other fruits like cooked prunes.*

### INGREDIENTS:
1 cup boiling water
1 cup raisins or cranberries
2 tablespoons shortening
1 large egg
½ cup sugar
½ cup molasses
1-1/2 cups flour
1 teaspoon salt
1 teaspoon baking soda, mixed with 1 tablespoon water

### DIRECTIONS:
Generously grease or butter a 1- quart pudding mold, empty coffee can or other pan that will fit into a covered pan for steaming. In medium bowl, combine the water, raisins or cranberries and shortening and let stand for five minutes, until shortening is melted. In another bowl, beat together the egg, sugar and molasses and stir into the raisin mixture. Add the flour, salt and baking soda mixture and stir well. Pour mixture into prepared pan and steam for two hours. Serve warm with hard sauce.

# Hard Sauce

### INGREDIENTS:
1 stick (1/2 cup) butter or margarine, softened
1-1/2 cups confectioner's (powdered) sugar
½ teaspoon vanilla
1 teaspoon dark rum, if desired

Combine all ingredients in a small mixing bowl and beat until smooth. Store, covered tightly, in refrigerator until ready to use.

# How to steam a pudding

If you don't have a steamer, you can use a Dutch oven or other deep kettle that holds enough water to last through the steaming process. You need a steamer insert or rack with holes in the bottom so the pudding mold or pan does not touch the bottom, and a tight fitting cover. Fill the greased pudding mold (you can use a 6-cup bundt pan or similar pan) no more than 2/3 full, to allow room for the batter to rise. Cover loosely with wax paper or parchment paper and secure paper to prevent water from dripping on pudding during steaming. Place the pan in the kettle on rack; add enough water to come about 2/3 of the way up the side of the pudding pan. Bring the water to a boil, then reduce to a low simmer, and cover tightly. Cook for required time, then remove pudding mold. Cool 10 minutes. Use a rubber spatula to loosen the pudding at one side and then invert onto serving dish.

# Coconut Cream (Coconut Jello)

*You will still see this favorite old Caymanian recipe on the table at East End parties and functions today. It has been handed down for generations, from a time when sweets were a special treat made from whatever we had on hand. I have never heard of anything like it from any other country.*

### INGREDIENTS:
3 envelopes unflavored Knox gelatin
½ cup cold water
½ cup boiling water
4 cups coconut milk*
1 14-ounce can plus 2 tablespoons condensed milk
½ cup grated coconut (optional)

### DIRECTIONS:
In a medium bowl, sprinkle gelatin over cold water and allow to soften. Add the boiling water and stir until gelatin is completely dissolved. Combine the condensed milk and coconut milk and stir until smooth, then add to gelatin. Mix well and stir in coconut, if desired. Refrigerate until set, about four hours. Top with stewed guava, diced mango or pineapple for a special dessert.

(* If using canned coconut milk instead of home made, use one can plus enough water to make 4 cups of coconut milk for this recipe).

# Pineapple Upside Down Cake

*This is still a very popular old-time dessert in Cayman. Even today, no party or local food sale is complete without it. There are many recipes for this cake and even a cake mix now too. This is an old recipe but still a very good one.*

*10-inch ovenproof skillet (cast iron is best) or heavy 9-inch cake pan*

### TOPPING:
5 tablespoons butter
1/2 cup light brown sugar, packed
9 canned pineapple rings, drained
9 maraschino cherries, drained

### CAKE:
1-1/3 cups flour
2 teaspoons baking powder
½ teaspoon salt
1 cup sugar
5 tablespoons unsalted butter, softened or 1/3 cup solid Crisco
1 large egg, beaten
1 teaspoon vanilla
2/3 cup milk
3 tablespoons dark rum for top

### DIRECTIONS:
Preheat oven to 350 F. Make the topping first. Melt the butter over medium high heat in a cast iron skillet or 9-inch heavy cake pan over medium heat and use a pastry brush to brush some of the butter up the sides. Sprinkle the brown sugar evenly over the melted butter on the bottom and reduce heat to low, to allow sugar to just melt, about 2 minutes, stirring until blended with butter. Remove skillet or pan from heat and arrange pineapple slices in concentric circles, overlapping slightly, over the bottom, placing a cherry in center of each.

**Make the cake batter:** Sift together the flour, baking powder and salt in medium bowl. In large mixing bowl, beat the butter or shortening until light, then blend in the sugar until smooth. Add the egg and mix well, then blend in the vanilla. Add the flour mixture alternately with the milk, blending well after each addition. Spoon the batter over the topping in the pan and bake in center of oven at 350 for 35-40 minutes or until toothpick inserted in center comes out clean.

Remove from oven and allow to cool five minutes, then invert a plate over the skillet, using oven mitts to hold it firmly in place. Turn the skillet upside down to turn the cake onto the plate. Replace any pineapple pieces stuck to the skillet or pan. Move the cake plate to a wire rack to cool and sprinkle 3 tablespoons rum over the top if desired. *Cool until warm before serving.*

# *Harris Griffiths Conolly's Christmas Fruit Cake*

*My brother Harris was the fifth of us children and a very good cook later in life. He was a seaman and worked as a chef on National Bulk Carriers. Here in Cayman, people loved his Christmas cakes, but he never wrote down the recipe. I remember what he used and how the cake tasted, and have done this recipe using the modern convenience of a food processor.*

### THE SOAKED FRUITS:
1 pound (2-3/4 cups) cups dark raisins or sultanas
2 cups golden raisins
1 pound (2-1/2 cups) currants or pitted dates
1 pound (2-1/4 cups) pitted prunes
2 cups glace cherries
2 cups mixed candied citrus peel
Rum, Port wine or Brandy

### DIRECTIONS:
In a food processor, grind together both raisins or sultanas, currants and prunes to form a thick paste. Combine with remaining fruits in a large crock or glass container with a tight seal and add enough rum, port wine, brandy or mixture of all, to cover by at least an inch. Soak at least 4 months, preferably 9 months, adding more liquor as the fruits absorb it, so they are always covered by at least a little alcohol. Traditionally, you would keep a crock of soaked fruits going year round, replenishing as you used.

### INGREDIENTS:
1 pound margarine
3-1/2 cups brown sugar
10 large eggs
2 tablespoons vanilla
4 cups flour
1 tablespoon baking powder
1 teaspoon ground nutmeg or mace
1 teaspoon ground cloves
1 teaspoon allspice
2 teaspoons cinnamon
1/4 cup browning (Kitchen Bouquet)
2 cups (1 pint) rum, brandy or red wine

**DIRECTIONS:**

Preheat oven to slow, 275 degrees. Line bottom and sides of 2-10-inch springform pans first with a layer of greased heavy brown paper, and then with two layers of greased waxed paper. This is important to seal in the rum and liquor that saturates the cake while aging.

Cream together margarine and sugar until light, then beat in eggs, one at a time. Blend in vanilla. In a separate bowl, sift together flour, baking powder and dry spices. Gradually add this to creamed mixture, blending until smooth. Stir in the fruits, then add the browning. Blend well. (If dipping into the crock, measure out the combined amount of soaked fruits above, about 3 quarts or 12 cups.)

Bake about 3 to 3-1/2 hours until wooden skewer inserted in center comes out with only a few crumbs clinging to it, but basically clean. Remove from oven and prick cakes top all over with skewer. While still hot, pour 1/2 cup rum or preferred liquor over each cake, a little at a time, (cakes will sizzle) until all has been absorbed, saturating them in the pan. Add more alcohol if you want. Let cool several hours at room temperature in the pan, then remove cakes and wrap tightly in cheesecloth soaked with rum or brandy. Wrap tightly in heavy aluminum foil or store in airtight containers. Open every week, unwrap and pour a little more rum or wine into holes and on cheesecloth if necessary so the cakes stay moist while aging.

# Nigga (Nigger?) Bible

*This is a simple recipe from poor times many years ago that used what was on hand to make a treat for the family. Some say it is a cake, others call it a bread. I can't tell you how it got its name and there are a lot of different recipes for it. If you had raisins, that made it extra special.*

**INGREDIENTS:**

2 cups brown sugar
¾ cup Crisco or margarine
2 cups water
3 cups flour
1 teaspoon baking soda

1 tablespoon baking powder
1 teaspoon salt
1 teaspoon ground cinnamon
1/4 teaspoon nutmeg
Raisins

**DIRECTIONS:**

Preheat oven to 350 F. Lightly grease and dust with flour a 9 x 13 inch pan. In a saucepan, mix brown sugar, water and shortening or margarine. Bring to a boil, stirring several times until smooth. Let cool.

In large bowl, combine dry ingredients and mix to blend. Stir in wet sugar mixture, just until blended. Pour into prepared pan and if using raisins, scatter them evenly over the top. Bake at 350 F for 30 minutes, or until wooden pick inserted in center of cake comes out clean. Do not over bake or it will be too dry!

# Guava

Years ago we didn't know how good guava is for you. We liked them because they grew wild and were one of the sweet fruits we had plenty of in East End. Stewed or "cut" guava and guava jam are old favorites. We would eat the whole fruit, skin and all, but the smell of ripe guavas is something you have to get used to!

# Cut Guava

*This is an old family recipe from my sister Olga. It is like jam, eaten as a spread on fresh bread. It is delicious!*

### INGREDIENTS:
5 pounds ripe guava
8 cups water
3 cups white sugar
3 cups water
½ teaspoon cinnamon
½ teaspoon red food coloring
¼ cup lime juice or ¼ teaspoon alum

### DIRECTIONS:
Peel the guava and cut in halves, then remove seeds. In a large pot or Dutch oven, combine the guava halves and 8 cups water and bring to a boil over medium high heat. Cook for 15-20 minutes, until soft, then strain guava and discard the water. Add 3 cups fresh water to the pot with the guava, then the sugar, cinnamon, food coloring and lime juice or alum and stir well. Bring to a boil then reduce heat to medium low and simmer slowly, stirring occasionally, until mixture has cooked down and is desired thickness.

# Guava Jelly

*First you have to make guava juice. Choose firm, ripe guavas and wash, cut off the ends and slice. Place in a large pot with just enough water to cover. Bring to a boil and reduce heat to medium high to keep at a low boil. Book until fruit is very soft, about 20 minutes. Drain the fruit through a strainer, mashing down to force the juice into a bowl beneath. You can use the leftover pulp for sauce or other recipes.*

### INGREDIENTS:
**4 cups guava juice**
**4 cups sugar**
**Juice of 2 large fresh limes**

### DIRECTIONS:
In a large saucepan or pot, bring the guava juice to a boil, then stir in the sugar and lime juice and mix well. Reduce heat and cook mixture slowly at a low boil, stirring often until sugar dissolves, until it thickens and a drop or two in cold water form a soft ball. Remove from heat and pour into sterilized jars and seal immediately.

# Guava Jam

Peel guavas and place in a large pot with just enough water to cover. Bring to a boil and cook until very soft. Drain and rub through a sieve until only the seeds are left. Discard seeds.

Pour the pulp into a medium saucepan or pot. For each cup of pulp, add ¾ cup sugar and a few squeezes of fresh lime juice to sharpen the flavor. Stir and bring to a boil, then reduce heat to a low boil and cook until mixture is thick. Pour into sterilized jars and seal immediately, or pour into bowl for immediate use. Refrigerate if not using right away, as it will spoil quickly.

# Sorrel Drink

*This is an old time Christmastime drink in Cayman that came from Jamaica. Some claim it helps fight the flu and cures fevers too. Our sorrel is actually a kind of hibiscus plant that blooms once a year in late fall. In December, you'll find packages of the dried blossoms that look like rose buds for sale in local supermarkets. Many people like to make enough to keep bottle hidden away for special occasions year round. It makes a nice punch even if you don't add rum.*

**INGREDIENTS:**
4 cups dried sorrel sepals (flowers)
2 pieces cinnamon stick or 4 teaspoons ground cinnamon
12 whole cloves
2 tablespoons grated fresh ginger
2 cups brown sugar
2 quarts boiling water
White or light rum or to taste, if desired

**DIRECTIONS:**
Remove the seeds from the sorrel and place sorrel, cinnamon, cloves, ginger and sugar in a large pot and cover with boiling water. Cool and let stand, loosely covered for two or three days at room temperature. Strain the liquid into another container, discard the solids and add rum if desired. Let sit, covered, for two days longer to age. Makes about 2 quarts. Store in refrigerator and serve chilled or over ice.

# Real Old Time Cayman Ice Cream

*This is "the real thing" and it is delicious. I have been making ice cream for over 25 years. I used to make it every November to sell with the poppies for Veteran's Day drive and in July for the annual Gun Bay United Church fundraiser on Constitution Day. Today I have to let the younger people do the work, but they still use my recipe. And people come from all over just to taste old fashioned ice cream. They can't make it fast enough!*

**INGREDIENTS:**
4 cans evaporated milk
3 cans condensed milk
1 teaspoon salt
1 cup of boiled cornstarch
¼ cup vanilla flavoring
White sugar to taste

**DIRECTIONS:**
The cornstarch is important and it must be thin, like Jell-O that is starting to set, not thick and hard. You make it from mixing 3 tablespoons cornstarch mixed with 1 cup water, then bring to a boil, stirring constantly. If mixture is too thick, stir in a little more water. There should be no lumps, and you will need to strain the mixture if necessary.

Mix all ingredients together in the freezer bucket, then cover bucket and proceed with the directions for the machine you are using---most ice cream freezers are electric today, but we always made this with a hand cranked freezer and it would take an hour of cranking!

# Cleo's Favorite Meal

*"What is your favorite meal?" friends asked Cleo as her 80th birthday approached. The answer might surprise you. Of Cayman's bounty of sophisticated cuisine or traditional dishes to choose from today, Cleo's favorite meal is a plate of stewed whelks with rice and beans. What would make it perfect would be a piece of steamed white Cayman Brac yam and slice of roast yellow-flesh breadfruit.*

Yes, I do love stew whelks! There used to be plenty of whelks here in East End. We could pick buckets of them off on Collier's Reef. There was a little Cay off the public beach there and that was a good place too. They were everywhere.

We children would go out and pick them off the reef at low tide, and sometimes along the rocky beaches too. But are they a lot of work! After you pick a pail full, then you must boil them, and then pick them out of the shell. Then you have to clean them: cut away the piece of shell at the end of the foot (operculum), and take off the guts and fat and peel off the tough black skin. Then you must grind them or use a sharp knife to cut them into very small pieces. Then you make coconut milk and cook them in that with, scallion, sweet green pepper and a little Cayman pepper. But the vegetables must be minced fine and cooked down…like you make stew conch.

Yes, they were plentiful years ago, but not today. Miss Vivine (Watler) cooks them down the road at her restaurant in Gun Bay when she can get some sent across from Cayman Brac and her recipe is very good.

*But her birthday is May 28 and whelk season is closed. The next best thing?*

Shrimps! We didn't have shrimps in East End when I was a child of course. But I like just plain boiled shrimps: no butter, no sauce, and no lime. I like the taste of them just the way they are. But now if you could find an ocean turbot and steam that for me, that would be nice too!"

*Cleo's favorite birthday cake? It wasn't cheesecake, carrot cake or coconut cake or any of the recipes that delighted her guests at Tortuga Club, or members of her Church.*

Cassava heavy cake, and my brother Frank makes the best. When I was a little girl, we would have a pot cake for our birthdays. That was like a heavy cake, and my favorite was made with bottlers. You could also make it with cassava, yam, even pumpkin. It was "baked" in the iron pot in the caboose. Oh was that good!

Frank makes the heavy cakes in our family, not me. He makes very good ones. People like them because they are just right---not hard but not too chewy, and just the right sweetness. People are always asking him to bake for parties and church functions.

# Stew Whelks, East End Style

*You have to boil the whelks first, and then pick the meat out of the shell. You can't get them out of the shell any other way unless you smash the whelk, which just makes a big fat mess. Cayman sea pie is an important part of this dish too.*

**INGREDIENTS:**
2 dozen large whelks, scrubbed
3 coconuts
8 cups water
1 medium sweet green pepper, chopped
1 large onion, chopped
½ teaspoon thyme
1 yellow Cayman pepper (Scotch bonnet) seeded and minced fine (to taste)
Salt and ground black pepper to taste

**SEA PIE:**
3 cups flour
½ teaspoon salt
1-1/2 cups water

**DIRECTIONS:**
Place whelks in a large stock pot or Dutch oven with enough water to cover and bring to a boil. Skim off any foam that rises and reduce heat to simmer. Cook about 30 minutes. Drain and allow whelks to cool until they can be handled, then pick out the snail and cut off the round shell at the end of the foot (the operculum) and the fat. In batches, grind the whelks coarse with the onion and sweet pepper and set aside in a bowl.

Make coconut milk: remove the meat from the coconut and cut in small pieces. Place in blender or food processor with the 8 cups of water and process until pureed and coconut is fine enough to strain the liquid from the "trash" using a sieve or mesh strainer. Pour the coconut milk into a large stockpot and bring to a boil. Reduce heat and keep at a medium boil until oil begins to appear on the surface, about 30 minutes. Add 3 more cups of water, stir well, then add thyme, Cayman pepper and ground whelks. Stir well, and then reduce heat to a low simmer. Cook until liquid has reduced by two thirds or to desired thickness, about an hour. During the last 20 minutes, add the sea pie.

# What are Whelks

What we call "wilks" or whelks, are not whelks at all, but Cittarium pica, the West Indian top shell, a marine mollusk with a striped black and white turban-shaped shell that thrives in rocky coastline just at the tidal line. Once abundant along Cayman's ironshore and shallow reefs, whelks are hard to find today and protected by our Marine Conservation laws (see below.)

Whelks are protected by Cayman's Marine Conservation Laws. Closed season is May 1 to October 31 and no one may take or purchase whelks from Cayman waters during those months. During open season, the catch limit is two and a half gallons in the shell, or two and a half pounds of cleaned whelks per person, per day.

# Cayman Sea Pie

The real name is "see pie" because the dough should be so thin you can "see through" it.

In a medium bowl, combine the flour and salt and slowly stir in enough water, about 1-1/2 cups water, to form soft dough which will be a little lumpy. Knead until it comes together, then stretch and roll out on a floured board with a rolling pin into a thin sheet—the dough should be so thin you can "spy through it" and cut into strips, and then into 1 inch pieces. Lay strips on top of simmering stew and cover; cook until firm but not hard, about 20 minutes. Add salt and black pepper to taste before serving.

# Rice and Beans, Cayman Style

*I don't make this for myself alone these days because you can't make "just a little" of this dish! Every cook has his own recipe and advice about how to make this dish come up nice and fluffy. Using long grain rice, not parboiled or converted rice, is important. You will just have to practice in your own kitchen. Homemade coconut milk makes a big difference too, but today, most people used canned coconut milk. Some cook the beans in coconut milk and if you do this, you have to adjust the amount of coconut milk called for. Some add onion, garlic and green pepper too And, like many other "simple" Caribbean dishes, it takes practice and patience to get your own recipe right. Adding a pinch of baking soda to the beans helps take out the gassiness.*

## INGREDIENTS:
1 cup dried red kidney beans or small red beans
¼ teaspoon baking soda
2 cups coconut milk (preferably freshly made)
2 cups white long grain rice
2 large scallions, chopped (green and white parts)
½ teaspoon black pepper
½ teaspoon dried thyme or 1 sprig of fresh thyme
2 teaspoons salt
1 seasoning pepper *(see note)

## DIRECTIONS:
Place the beans and baking soda in a large (3-quart or larger) heavy saucepan or aluminum Dutch oven (called a caldero) and add enough water to cover. Soak overnight. (Or use the quick soak method: bring beans to a full boil and boil for two minutes, then remove from heat and let soak for an hour. Then proceed as follows):

When ready to prepare the recipe, bring the beans to a boil and cover, then reduce heat to simmer. Cook the beans for an hour or until tender, adding water if necessary to keep beans covered. Never add salt to bean water before or during cooking or it will toughen them. Once the beans are tender, drain and reserve 2-3/4 cups of the bean broth, adding more water to make up that amount if necessary.

Return the beans and the 2-3/4 cups bean broth to the pot. Pour in the coconut milk, scallion, thyme, seasoning pepper, salt and black pepper. Bring to a boil and simmer five minutes, then add the rice, stirring while adding. After you add the rice there should be about ½ inch of liquid covering the mixture—add more coconut milk or water if necessary. When the pot returns to a boil, reduce heat to low and cover tightly. Do not stir again until rice is done. Check after 15 minutes and if rice appears too firm and liquid has been absorbed, add about 1/3 cup more water and cover again. Repeat if necessary until the rice has absorbed all the liquid and is light and fluffy—about 25 –35 minutes. It should not be mushy. Remove from heat, keep covered and let rest for 10 minutes before serving.

## What are Seasoning Peppers?

In Cayman, our local "seasoning peppers" are small, flatter relatives of the Scotch Bonnet and have much of the same flavor without the heat. They are unique to Cayman and easy to find in Grand Cayman's local supermarket produce sections, but not available overseas. You can add a few slivers of seeded Scotch Bonnet or other hot pepper, or a few drops of hot pepper sauce if you like it.

# Frank Conolly's
# Cassava Heavy Cake

Frank makes the heavy cakes in our family, not me. He makes very good ones. Many people in East End say his are the best! They like them because they are just right---not hard but not too chewy either, and just the right sweetness. People are always asking him to bake for parties and church functions.

As Frank himself explained, this is another recipe whose primary ingredient isn't even mentioned: a Caymanian cook's intuition and the ability to "cook by eye."

"I can't give you exact times now, you know. You have to watch the cake and know when it's ready at each step. It's not easy, and it takes some time and prctice to learn how to make a heavy cake. You can use canned coconut milk, but homemade coconut milk is best." Frank said.

## INGREDIENTS:
6 pounds grated cassava (you can buy it frozen in supermarkets)
3 large dry coconuts
1 gallon water
4 pounds dark brown sugar
1 pound butter or margarine, softened
2 teaspoons salt
2 teaspoons mixed spice (nutmeg and cinnamon)
3 tablespoons cornstarch
3 tablespoons water
3 cups water

## DIRECTIONS:
If using frozen cassava, make sure it is thawed. Pry the coconut meat from the shell and peel off the brown skin, then cut the white meat, into small pieces. Put coconut in blender or food processor and process until fine. Make the coconut milk by combining the meat and 1 gallon water in batches in a blender, blending well, and then straining the mixture through a strainer into a large (8 quart) pot. Throw away the trash –feed it to the chickens if you have them.

Put the pot on to boil and keep coconut milk at a low boil, uncovered, until oil forms on the top, about an hour. Slowly stir in the sugar, then the butter or margarine and mix until blended. Bring the mixture back to a boil, then reduce the heat to an even boil and boil down until thick, about an hour longer. Remove 1 cup of the mixture as basting juice and set aside. Blend the cornstarch and 3 tablespoons water to make a smooth paste and stir into the cassava mixture. Then add the 3 cups water and mix until blended well, then add the salt and spice. Continue boiling the coconut mixture until very thick, about an hour longer. Turn off heat and prepare baking pan.

Preheat oven to 350 and have a large baking pan, 14 x 21 inches waiting. Pour enough of the reserved juice into the bottom of the pan and heat in oven until it turns dark brown and begins to caramelize—about 15 minutes. Do not allow to burn!

Remove pan from oven and pour the cake batter into the pan and bake for 1 hour. Remove and baste the top generously with some of the remaining juice. Bake another hour at 350, then baste again with remaining juice. Reduce heat to 200 and bake 1 hour longer (total baking time is about 3 hours.)

Remove from oven and cool. Do not cover cake until completely cool and do NOT store in the refrigerator. Heavy cake must be served at room temperature. If you worry about ants, cover the cake with aluminum foil tightly and it will keep for a week.

# Papaya Heavy Cake

## INGREDIENTS:
6 pounds of green papaya, peeled and seeded
6 dry coconuts
6 quarts water
4 pounds dark brown sugar
1 pound butter, softened
3 teaspoons spice (nutmeg and cinnamon) or to taste
1 teaspoon salt
3 cups cornstarch

## DIRECTIONS:
Cut up the peeled papaya and place in a large pot with enough water to cover. Boil until soft, then drain well and mash fine. Set aside.

Pry the coconut meat from the shell and peel off the brown skin, then cut the white meat into small pieces. Put the coconut in a blender or food processor and process until fine. Make the coconut milk by combining the meat and water in batches in a blender, blending well, and then straining the mixture through cheesecloth into a large (8 quart) pot.

Put the coconut milk in the pot and bring to a boil, then reduce heat and keep at a low boil, uncovered, until oil forms on the top. Slowly stir in the sugar, then the butter or margarine, spice and salt mix until blended. Return to a low boil and remove 1 cup of the liquid to use as basting juice.

Mix together the papaya and cornstarch and stir into the coconut mixture. Lower the heat to a very low boil and cook down until the batter is very thick, about two hours, stirring occasionally.

Preheat oven to 350. Have a 14 x 21 pan ready. Spread enough of the reserved basting liquid on the bottom of the pan to grease it. Pour the cake batter into the greased pan and bake for an hour, until the top has browned. Remove pan and baste the top with the remaining liquid. Bake an hour longer, or until cake has a smooth firm texture and a knife inserted in center comes out clean.

## Heavenly Cayman Heavy Cake

Heavy cake is a traditional favorite Caymanian sweet, another very old recipe that illustrates the resourcefulness of cooks when ingredients were scarce and expensive. There are many varieties, including cassava, yam, cornmeal, sweet potato, green papaya —even biscuit (crackers), but cassava remains the favorite. It's also a recipe that has resisted streamlining by modern conveniences like the microwave. With the exception of blenders and food processors that speed up making coconut milk, heavy cake is still an all day labor of love in today's world of instant everything. And Caymanian men make some of the best, including Miss Cleo's brother Frank, and she is quick and generous with her praise for his culinary accomplishments as the King of East End heavy cakes.

# Part Two

# Miss Cleo's Kitchen
## Recipes From
## Around the World at
## Tortuga Club

# Introduction
## Miss Cleo's International Cuisine at Tortuga Club

The hand written menus and recipes from Miss Cleo's old black and white school composition notebooks revealed many surprises. During more than 30 years as head chef at Tortuga Club, her guests were treated to an unexpected range of recipes for a remote island resort kitchen. In addition to Caymanian recipes adapted to please foreign tastes, Cleo's dinner menu might feature dishes from England, Germany or France. American and Canadian guests were surprised to find favorite comfort foods from home too. Miss Cleo served dishes from every region in the USA: home-style chicken and dumplings and pot roast from America's heartland; Yankee favorites like pot roast and corned beef and cabbage; cornbread and fried chicken from down south in Dixie.

Every night was a feast from around the world, which began with homemade soups and freshly baked breads and ended with memorable pies and desserts missed by many of her friends today.

Miss Cleo explained: "During the first years at Tortuga Club, there were no printed menus for the dining room. Each night, the waitresses would come to every table and read the selections for guests off a piece of paper I had written. All of our staff was from East End, and sometimes they had difficulties pronouncing the names of the dishes. And with their broad Caymanian accents, well sometimes this left guests shaking their heads and wondering what on earth those things were that they would be served! Well, let me tell you: that's the way it is today for me, when I read some of the confusion and things on restaurant menus. I don't know what to think!"

Miss Cleo always speaks her mind. She has no hesitation about setting you straight about things culinary --and life in general. That's also the way she ran HER kitchen at Tortuga Club until she retired. You could leave your opinions at the door.

Around 1982 the new owners of Tortuga Club dared to interfere in her kitchen and threatened to disrupt Miss Cleo's routine. This was the time when the global soybean industry, in the guise of an army of generously rewarded medical "experts," launched its campaign against tropical oils. Palm, coconut and other natural oils were targeted as treacherous, heart-crippling substances. Cayman's traditional coconut cuisine was suddenly dangerous and unacceptable for tourists. The owners of Tortuga Club told Cleo to stop using coconuts.

Cleo was quite direct, to put it mildly. In her famous, declarative East End brogue, she told them, "What?!!??? You not taking away my coconuts! If coconut is so bad then tell me why there are so many 90 year old people here in Cayman today? In days gone, sometimes that's all we had. Now tell me how am I going to cook our food without it!!? This is my kitchen and I am going to keep cooking with coconut until you fire me."

Miss Cleo won that battle.

*Cleo's Island Cookery Tips*

### How to make breadcrumbs and bread cubes

Don't be ashamed to admit you don't know how to make homemade breadcrumbs. Convenience foods have erased that from almost every cook's memory.

**For dry breadcrumbs,** it's important that the bread be several days old and firm or dry-- as bread gets after a few days. Or you can dry bread in the oven if it's fresh. It should NOT be stale (or worse, moldy) please! That word stale has been used incorrectly for too long!

If you have only soft fresh bread, toast it lightly first to dry out, tear the bread into smaller pieces, place in a food processor or blender, and pulse until desired texture of coarseness. Of, if you want to be old fashioned, use a box grater.

Tip: You can make up a batch of breadcrumbs and freeze them in plastic Ziploc bags too—just be sure to squeeze all the air out of the Ziploc bag before freezing so trapped moisture doesn't form ice crystals. They will keep for a month in the freezer.

### Rule of thumb for measuring breadcrumbs is:

2 standard slices fresh bread = 1 cup soft breadcrumbs
3 standard slices bread, day old or dry = 1 cup dry bread crumbs

**For bread cubes:** If you are making bread pudding or breakfast casseroles (stratas) that call for bread cubes, you can use fresh bread, simply chop the bread into small pieces using a sharp knife, or use a food processor to make fine crumbs. The measure is:

1 standard slice fresh bread = about 1 cup soft bread cubes
1 standard slice dry bread = about 1/2 cup bread cubes.

### If you are using buttered breadcrumbs for a gratin or casserole topping:

Delicious homemade buttered breadcrumbs can add great flavor to simple dishes.

They are easy to make: melt 4 tablespoons butter in a medium skillet over medium heat, then sprinkle over ½ to 1-1/2 cups dry breadcrumbs—the amount of breadcrumbs used depends on how rich and buttery you want your crumb topping. Stir quickly to coat crumbs, and continue stirring until they start to turn golden brown. Remove from heat and use as topping.

**For garlic breadcrumbs:** add 1/8 teaspoon minced fresh garlic or ¼ teaspoon garlic powder for every 1-1/2 cups of crumbs to butter before adding crumbs.

**For cheese breadcrumbs:** add ¼ cup grated parmesan or other hard cheese for every 1-1/2 cups crumbs when adding the crumbs to the butter.

**Baking dish sizes:**

It's often confusing when recipes call for quarts instead of inch sizes in baking dish sizes. Use this guide:

| | | |
|---|---|---|
| **1-1/2 – 2 quart baking dish** | = | **8 x 8 x 2 or 7 x 11 inch casserole or pan** |
| **3 quart baking dish** | = | **9 x 13 x 2 inch casserole or pan** |
| **4 quart baking dish** | = | **10 x 15 x 2 inch casserole or pan** |
| **5-6 quart baking dish** | = | **12 x 20 x 2 (catering or crowd size!)** |

**Wash your meat, chicken and seafood!!** Not cleaning your fish, chicken and other meat is one of the biggest mistakes chefs make today, especially in the islands. Use white vinegar or fresh lime juice and cold water to "wash" away any blood, stale juices and foulness and freshen the meats. This is best done using a large bowl and pouring over a small amount of vinegar or lime juice mixed with cold water, making sure all the surfaces are soaked for several minutes, then rinsing in cold water again. Do not let fish or shellfish stand in lime juice or vinegar for long or they will "cook" and become soft and mushy.

**Learn to make a white or cream sauce.** It is the base for many recipes, especially seafood dishes.

**Basic Cream Sauce**

A simple cream sauce, properly seasoned to suit the other ingredients, can transform a simple dish into something special. This is also the basic recipe for the binder for savory casseroles and pot pies. You can double or quadruple these measurements depending on your needs.

**2 tablespoons butter**
**2 tablespoons flour**
**1 cup evaporated milk or light cream**
**Salt and pepper to taste**

In a small skillet, melt the butter over medium heat then sprinkle over the flour. Blend well with a wooden spoon so there are no lumps, then continue stirring slowly and cook one minute, until flour is no longer raw. Do not let it brown. Slowly add the cream, stirring constantly and cook until sauce is thickened. Stir in salt and pepper to desired taste.

**Add slices of green papaya to tenderize roasts and stews.** Peel and cut slices of green papaya, including the seeds and lay slices on top of a roast before cooking. Some say you should peel, cut up and boil a small green papaya, seeds and all, and allow to cool, then pour this over raw meat like a marinade as a tenderizer. I think adding the green papaya slices works better.

**Watch your spices and check them before using!** The nose is the best judge. This is very important in the Caribbean where heat and humidity can make herbs and spices go rancid quickly. Check them as soon as you buy them and return if they are old! Dry herbs and spices, especially expensive ones like paprika, can go off quickly in tropical climate of an island kitchen, or if they were sitting too long on the market shelf. Cooking with stale spices will ruin a recipe and your reputation as a cook. Storing your spices in tightly closed containers in the refrigerator will help keep them fresh but even then, they should be replaced as soon as they even hint of staleness, after several months.

**Add fresh or dried green herbs, like thyme, rosemary, basil and oregano, during the last ten minutes of cooking.** If you have always added your spices earlier then try adding another pinch or two during the last ten minutes and you will find out the flavor is much brighter.

**Never let soups and stews boil.** Bring to a boil, then reduce fire or heat to a level that will let them simmer slowly. Keep them at a low simmer. Slow cooking develops the flavor and texture of these dishes.

**Thickening soups, sauces and stews:** there is nothing worse than a watery soup or stew that should be creamy or thick. You can thicken these dishes even as late as the last 5- 10 minutes of cooking by using cornstarch or flour. To thicken with flour, for every cup of liquid you need to thicken, mix 1 tablespoon of flour with 2 tablespoons water to form a paste. Stir a little of the hot soup or gravy into the paste and then stir this slowly into the pot until blended. Cook until mixture has thickened and the raw flour taste has cooked away, at least 5 minutes, adding more if not thick enough. Sauces thickened with flour will keep their consistency when reheated.

Cornstarch is newer to our cooking and it gives a silkier, glossy look to soups and stews. Use it as you would flour, dissolving first in water. Cornstarch has twice the thickening power of flour. Keep this in mind so you don't end up with a pot of jelly. But if you do, just keep cooking the soup. Cornstarch will break down if heated too high or too long, or if reheated. It is better for thickening sweets like puddings and pie fillings.

**Stop using so much tomato paste!** If you want to know how to season with this ingredient properly, taste a little right from the can and you will understand. A little goes a long way and it is often too sharp or vinegary to use in a recipe where a little ketchup would work better.

# Appetizers and Drinks

I don't drink spirits and did not work in the bar, so this chapter is very short. Bartending was my younger brother Frank Conolly's talent and one that won him several awards. Frank was General Manager of the Tortuga Club in the 1980s— but before that he managed the bar. He has his own stories to tell about that! His rum concoctions were famous, not only with resort guests— but also a fair number of prominent local customers who drove all the way from George Town and sometimes, could not drive back.

# Cayman Holiday

*This is Frank's legendary –and lethal--concoction from Tortuga Club.*

### INGREDIENTS:
3 ounces Myers Dark Rum
1 ounce Appleton Gold Rum
1 ounce Appleton Light Rum
1 ounce brandy
½ ounce Triple Sec or orange Curacao
1 ounce fresh lime or lemon juice
1 ounce strawberry syrup
1 ounce pineapple juice
1 ounce orange juice

### DIRECTIONS:
Combine all ingredients in a cocktail shaker with cracked ice and shake well—this is not a blender drink. Pour into a tall glass and sip slowly. Limit one per person, per night!

Those who ignored the house rule limiting bar guests to one Cayman Holiday did so at their own risk. One too many of Frank's rum drinks could leave even respected barristers and government officials imitating ostriches—according to Frank, literally: with their heads in the sand on Tortuga Club's beach after dark..

# Coconut Chips

This was my most famous appetizer which was served at the bar at "happy hour." Guests came looking for more when the bowls ran out. It is the easiest coconut snack possible.

Preheat oven to 350 F. Take one medium fresh brown coconut, crack and pry the meat from the shell in pieces that you can hold easily. Using a vegetable peeler or sharp paring knife (be careful!) peel away the thin brown skin, leaving white meat. Then peel the meat into long, thin, wide strips about an inch or so long.

Spread on a baking sheet or piece of aluminum foil, lightly salt the coconut and bake at 350 for about 10 minutes, or until just turning light golden brown. Be careful not to let the coconut turn too dark or it will be bitter! Remove and cool slightly, but serve warm. You won't have to worry about storing leftovers, but you will have to worry about keeping the bowls filled!

Hint: There is no need to spray these with vegetable oil spray, as some people today think, because the coconut oil in the fresh meat is enough.

Even coconuts have a shelf life: If you are having a hard time trying to pry the meat out of the shell and peeling the brown skin off the coconut meat, it is because the coconut is old. An uncracked brown coconut stays fresh for about 4 months.

# Homemade Breads

*I don't understand why many restaurants today don't serve fresh bread to guests waiting for their meal. It is one of the little courtesies that is always appreciated and sets the guests' mood right from the start. I always had at least one kind of fresh baked bread in a basket on the table for guests at dinner. Some were savory, some sweet. Here are recipes for favorite ones.*

# Simple English Scones

My freshly baked scones welcomed guests during a 4 p.m. island tea time at the original Tortuga Club. For many American guests, this was their first encounter with this traditional English custom. Scones should have a delicate, melt in your mouth texture--- not like the "rock cakes" sold in bakeries today, which are dense, hard floury wedges stuffed with currents or raisins.

If you want to add currants or raisins, do it right before you turn the dough out onto the work surface.

## INGREDIENTS:
2 cups flour
2 tablespoons sugar
2 teaspoons baking powder
½ teaspoon salt
¼ cup chilled unsalted butter, cut into small pieces
¾ cup whole milk
* 1/3 cup currants or raisins (optional)

## DIRECTIONS:
Preheat oven to 450 and make sure the upper rack is in the middle of the oven. Grease a baking sheet. Sift together dry ingredients (flour through salt) into a large mixing bowl. With pastry blender, two knives—or your fingertips, cut or work the butter into the flour mixture until mixture resembles coarse meal, with a few larger lumps. Make a well in the center of the flour mixture and add the milk. Blend ingredients quickly with wooden spoon or rubber spatula until a soft dough forms. Turn dough onto lightly floured surface.

If you want round scones, roll dough out until about ½ inch thick with lightly floured rolling pin and using a floured 3 inch biscuit or cookie cutter, cut out the scones. Dip biscuit cutter into flour as necessary to keep dough from sticking to it. Gather leftover dough and pat out ½ inch thick. Cut out scones until dough is used. Place scones about 2 inches apart on greased baking sheet and baking until light brown, about 10-12 minutes.

If you want wedge-shaped scones, turn the dough out onto lightly floured surface and with floured hands, gather dough and shape and pat it into a smooth round—do not over handle dough or scones will be tough. Cut round into eight wedges with a floured knife and transfer to greased baking sheet, placing about 2 inches apart. Bake as above. Serve warm with butter and jam.

# Cleo's Cayman Style Cornbread

*Guests at the Club could not seem to get enough of my cornbread. It was served every night with dinner.*

**INGREDIENTS:**
1-1/2 cups yellow cornmeal
¾ cup flour
¼ cup sugar
4 teaspoons baking powder
½ teaspoon salt
1-1/4 cups cream (evaporated milk)
2 large eggs, lightly beaten
½ cup margarine, melted

**DIRECTIONS:**
Preheat oven to 400 F. Grease or butter an 8 inch square baking pan. In a large mixing bowl, combine dry ingredients and blend with a fork or wire whisk. In separate bowl, mix together cream, eggs and margarine, then add all at once to dry ingredients. Mix just until blended, then pour batter into pan. Bake 20-25 minutes, until golden brown on top and knife inserted in center comes out clean—don't over bake or bread will be too dry. Cut into 9 squares.

# Cleo's Corn Muffins for 150

*You never know when someone might ask you to help with a party or a church event —or a chili cook-off. Or in my case, have a phone call from the chef of Tortuga Club asking for my recipe! If you want to please any crowd, bake a batch of fresh corn muffins. This simple recipe is still one of my best.*

### INGREDIENTS:
2 – 5 pound bags yellow cornmeal
1 – 5 pound bag flour (not self rising)
3-1/2 pounds sugar
30 tablespoons baking powder
6 teaspoons salt
1 gallon fresh whole milk
30 large eggs, beaten
1 pound butter, melted

### DIRECTIONS:
Preheat oven to 425 F. Lightly grease 4 -12-cup muffin tins. (You will need to bake these in batches.) In a bowl large enough to hold it, combine the cornmeal, flour, sugar, baking powder and salt. Whisk with wire whisk or large fork until dry ingredients are blended. Combine the eggs, milk and butter and stir into the cornmeal mixture, just until blended and no lumps remain. Fill muffin tins 2/3 full and bake at 425 F for 15 minutes, or until tops are golden brown. Remove muffins from oven and cool slightly, but serve warm, with butter.

# Popovers

Four ingredients, that's all-and NO baking powder or soda! This is a very a simple recipe-but ingredients should be at room temperature. Popovers take time to bake properly to reach their puffed high hat shape. My recipe uses "cream" or evaporated milk, which makes them even richer. If you don't own a hand rotary beater, use an electric mixer on low speed but do not over beat!

### INGREDIENTS:
4 large eggs
2 cups evaporated milk or whole milk
2 cups flour
1 teaspoon salt

### INGREDIENTS:
Preheat oven to 450 F. Butter very well 8 large (6 ounce) custard cups. You can use a large 6-cup muffin tin but take care to butter each space. Arrange the custard cups in a pan large enough to hold all without letting them slide around.

Using a hand rotary beater or electric mixer on low speed, beat eggs lightly, then add milk and add flour and salt and beat just until batter is smooth-do not over mix. Pour batter into prepared cups to ¾ full.

Bake popovers for 25 minutes at 450 F , then reduce oven to 350 F and bake another 15 to 20 minutes, until deep golden brown and puffed, then remove from cups right away onto wire rack, using spatula or knife if necessary-this prevents bottoms from becoming soggy. Serve immediately with butter.

- If you want firm popovers with crispy tops instead of puffy, custardy ones, cut a slit inside of each to let out steam then bake another 8-10 minutes.

# Yorkshire Pudding

This is a traditional English dish to serve with roast beef-usually a standing or boneless prime rib roast. About 30 minutes before the roast is done, make the batter for Yorkshire Pudding. The batter will rise high during baking, then deflate to create a custardy center and crisp, puffed edges that is cut into squares and served hot.

## INGREDIENTS:
2 large eggs
1 cup milk
1 cup flour
½ teaspoon salt

## DIRECTIONS:
Place a 8 x 8 x 2 inch square pan in the oven to heat. With a rotary beater or electric mixer on low, mix all ingredients just until smooth. Remove roast from oven and increase heat to 425 F. Pour off ½ cup drippings-if you don't have enough, add vegetable oil to make up the difference. Return meat to oven and let oven return to 425.

Pour the hot drippings in the hot pan and pour in the batter. Bake pudding for 10 minutes, then remove roast (and cover with foil) and bake pudding 25-30 minutes longer. Cut into square and serve hot with sliced roast and remaining au jus.

# Cleo's Quick Sally Lunn

Sally Lunn recipes date back to the 1800s and appeared in many old Southern US cookbooks, usually as a sweet yeast bread. Traditionally it was baked in a cast iron skillet greased with melted butter. The quicker, baking powder version became popular back in the 1950's. How did this recipe find its way to Cleo's East End kitchen?

*I found a recipe in a magazine and it looked good, but I changed it a little and added cinnamon! I loved to try new things, but usually added my own touches.*

### INGREDIENTS:
2 large eggs, beaten
1 cup whole milk
2 cups flour
2 teaspoons baking powder
1/3 cup sugar
1 teaspoon salt
¼ teaspoon cinnamon
6 tablespoons melted butter
Cinnamon sugar (1 tablespoon sugar mixed with 1/8 teaspoon cinnamon)

### DIRECTIONS:
Preheat oven to 350 F. Butter (use butter, not Crisco to grease!) a 9-inch square cake pan or 8 x 4 inch loaf pan. In a large mixing bowl, beat together eggs and milk. In a medium bowl, sift together flour, baking powder, sugar, salt and cinnamon. Gradually add the milk mixture just until blended, then stir in the melted butter. Pour into prepared pan and sprinkle top with cinnamon sugar. Bake for 40-45 minutes until golden brown on top or until toothpick inserted in center comes out clean. This is delicious anytime and even better toasted. You can also bake the batter in a 12-cup muffin tin, but reduce the baking time to 20 minutes.

## Tip from Cleo's Kitchen:

Bread slices neatly and easily by "sawing" back and forth if you use a serrated bread knife. Sometimes not even the sharpest straight knife in your kitchen will slice fresh baked bread properly and can ruin soft fresh crusty loaves. If you like bread, you should have one of these specialty knives in your drawer!

# Herb Bread

*Guests loved this bread, served warm from the oven. It fills the kitchen with a wonderful smell while it bakes-and taste as good as it smells! No kneading is necessary-but be sure to wet your hands before handling the batter.*

**INGREDIENTS:**
1-1/4 cups warm water (not boiling hot!)
1 envelope active dry yeast
2 tablespoons lard or Crisco solid vegetable shortening
2 tablespoons sugar
2 teaspoons salt
3 cups flour
1 teaspoon caraway seeds
½ teaspoon nutmeg
½ teaspoon sage
2 tablespoons butter, melted

**DIRECTIONS:**
In a large mixing bowl, dissolve the yeast in the warm water, then add lard or shortening, sugar and salt. Stir well until blended, then add 1-1/2 cups flour and the spices. Mix well with a wooden spoon (300 strokes!) or beat two minutes with electric mixer. Scrape the bottom and sides of bowl frequently. Add the remaining 1-1/2 cups flour and mix with spoon, scraping sides of bowl, making sure batter is blended well. Cover dough with a clean cloth or towel and let rise in warm place until doubled, about 30 minutes.

Grease well two 8-1/2 x 4-1/2 loaf pans. Beat the dough with spoon about 25 strokes, then divide dough evenly between the two prepared pans. Dough will be sticky, so smooth out the tops by lightly flouring your hand and patting down. Let dough rise again until it reaches ¼ inch from top of pans, about 40 minutes.

Heat oven to 375 F. Bake loaves 45-50 minutes, until tops are golden brown and bread sounds hollow when tapped lightly with a knife. Remove from oven and remove loaves from pans and cool on wire racks. Brush tops lightly with melted butter right away.

# Sensational Egg Bread

*That's how guests used to describe this bread. It is delicious warm from the oven, but some think it's even better toasted, especially served with mango jam from North Side. This recipe makes three loaves-it's best to make plenty because it will disappear fast.*

## INGREDIENTS:
½ cup warm water
2 packages active dry yeast
¼ cup lard, Crisco or butter
1-1/2 cups warm milk (lukewarm) **
¼ cup sugar
1 tablespoon salt
3 large eggs, beaten
7-1/4 – 7-1/2 cups sifted flour

## DIRECTIONS:
In an extra large mixing bowl, dissolve the yeast in warm water. Stir in the lard or butter, then add milk, sugar, salt and eggs, stirring well. Add 3-3/4 cups flour and mix until very smooth. Add enough remaining flour to make soft dough that you can handle easily. Turn dough out onto lightly floured board and knead until smooth, about 8-10 minutes. Cover with a clean cloth or towel and let rest and rise until doubled in size, about an hour.

Grease three 9 x 5 x 3 inch loaf pans. Divide dough into three portions. Shape dough into three loaves (flatten dough, then fold in half lengthwise and roll up-and place in pans sealed edge down-do not just lump dough into the pans.) Brush tops of loaves with additional shortening or softened butter. Cover again with cloth and let rise until sides reach top of pan and center is rounded, about another hour.

Heat oven to 425 F. Bake 25 to 30 minutes, until loaf tops are golden brown. Loaves should sound hollow when tapped. Remove from pans immediately and cool on wire racks.

*(** use ½ cup hot water and 1 cup evaporated milk, mixed together, if you want richer bread)*

# Old Time Biscuits

*Not many people make biscuits from scratch today, with so many mixes and frozen convenience foods. But nothing compares to the smell and taste of warm old time biscuits. They will make even a simple meal special.*

## INGREDIENTS:

2 cups flour
3 teaspoons baking powder
1 teaspoon salt
¼ cup Crisco solid shortening (not oil!)
¾ cup whole milk

## DIRECTIONS:

Preheat oven to 450 F. Combine flour, baking powder and salt in a large mixing bowl and stir with fork or wire whisk. Work the shortening into the flour mixture with your fingertips or pastry blender until it looks like coarse, pea-size crumbs. Gradually add the milk, stirring with a fork only until a soft dough forms and leaves the sides of the bowl. The dough should be puffy. Turn dough out onto lightly floured surface and knead just enough to make the dough come together nicely-about 10 times.

Lightly flour a rolling pin and roll dough out on lightly floured surface to about a thickness of a half inch. Cut out with a floured biscuit cutter or the bottom of a drinking glass. Place biscuits on lightly greased baking sheet (not a dark one or biscuits will be too brown) about an inch apart. Bake 10-12 minutes until golden brown.

# Onion Bread

*You will be surprised by the delicious flavor the fresh onion gives to this recipe! Don't use dried chopped or dehydrated minced onion flakes or it will ruin the bread.*

## INGREDIENTS:

1 cup warm whole milk
3 tablespoons sugar
1 teaspoon salt
2 tablespoons vegetable oil
2 envelopes dry yeast
¼ cup warm water
½ cup minced fresh onion
6 cups flour

### DIRECTIONS:

In a large mixing bowl, combine milk, sugar, salt and vegetable oil and stir until sugar is dissolved. In a small bowl, completely dissolve the yeast in the warm water, then stir into the milk mixture. Stir in the onions, then add enough flour to make a stiff dough; mix until dough is smooth. Cover with a clean soft cloth and let rise until doubled in bulk, about 45 minutes to an hour.

Grease or lightly oil two 9 x 5 inch loaf pans. When dough has risen, punch dough down and turn onto lightly floured board or surface. Divide dough in two and shape into smooth loaves. Place in pans and let rise again until doubled in bulk.

Preheat oven to 350 F. and bake loaves for 55 minutes to an hour, or until they sound hollow when tapped with finger or dull knife. Cool five minutes in pan then turn out onto wire rack to cool. This bread is best served warm, and will slice more easily if cooled 20 -30 minutes.

# Cheese- Garlic Biscuits

*Red Lobster restaurants are a Caymanian favorite when visiting Florida. One of the reasons is the baskets of warm cheese biscuits that come with every meal. If you like those cheese biscuits, try making these to surprise your family.*

### INGREDIENTS:
**4 cups Bisquick**
**1-1/3 cups milk**
**1 cup shredded sharp cheddar cheese (4 ounces)**
**¼ cup butter, melted**
**¼ teaspoon garlic powder or garlic salt**

### DIRECTIONS:

Preheat oven to 450ºF. In large mixing bowl, combine Bisquick mix and cheese and stir lightly, then add milk. Stir until soft dough forms. Drop dough by large tablespoonfuls onto ungreased cookie sheet. Bake 8 to 10 minutes or until golden brown. Combine melted butter and garlic powder; brush lightly over warm biscuits. Makes 16-18 biscuits, depending on how large you make them.

# Cleo's Cheese Nut Bread

*This is delicious right from the oven-but leftover bread, toasted, is good too.*

### INGREDIENTS:
3 cups flour
1 teaspoon salt
3 teaspoons baking powder
2 teaspoons sugar
½ teaspoon ground black pepper
1/2 teaspoon garlic powder
1/2 cup sunflower seeds
1 cup sharp cheddar cheese, shredded or crumbled
1-1/2 cups whole milk
¼ cup butter, melted
2/3 cup sour cream

### DIRECTIONS:
Preheat oven to 350. Grease or spray with Pam two 9 x 5 inch loaf pans, or a 10 cup bundt pan. In large mixing bowl, combine first seven dry ingredients and use fork or wire whisk to blend. Stir in cheese until evenly mixed. In medium bowl, mix together milk, butter and sour cream until smooth, then add to flour mixture, stirring just until ingredients are mixed and a thick batter forms Do not over mix! Spoon batter into prepared pans and bake 45-50 minutes, until golden brown on top and wooden pick inserted in center comes out clean. Cool bread in pan 5 minutes, then remove and cool on wire rack about 30-45 minutes before slicing.

# Banana Nut Bread

*When I see stores in Cayman throwing out boxes of very ripe bananas it grieves me because it is so wasteful. Those very ripe bananas can easily be made into these sweet and delicious breads.*

### INGREDIENTS:
1-3/4 cups flour
1/2 teaspoon salt
3/4 teaspoon baking soda
¼ teaspoon nutmeg
1/2 cup butter

1 cup sugar
2 large eggs
1 teaspoon vanilla extract
1 cup mashed very ripe bananas
1/3 cup evaporated milk
1/4 cup chopped walnuts
¼ cup raisins

## DIRECTIONS:

Preheat oven to 325 F. Lightly grease and flour bottom only of a 9 x 5 inch loaf pan. Combine flour, salt, baking soda and nutmeg and blend with a fork or wire whisk. In large mixing bowl, cream butter and sugar until light. Add eggs, one at a time, beating after each addition, then add vanilla, bananas and milk, mixing until smooth. Add flour mixture gradually and blend just until mixed. Stir in nuts or raisins. Spoon batter into prepared pan and bake at 325 for an hour, or until toothpick inserted in center comes out clean.

# Cayman Coconut Banana Bread

## INGREDIENTS:
1 cup butter or margarine
2 cups sugar
4 large eggs, beaten
2 cups mashed very ripe bananas (about 10 apple bananas or 5 medium imported ones)
2-1/4 cups flour
1 teaspoon salt
2 teaspoons baking soda
1/4 teaspoon nutmeg
1 cup grated fresh coconut

## DIRECTIONS:

Preheat oven to 350 F. Lightly grease and flour two 8 x 4 x 2 inch pans. In large mixing bowl, cream the butter and sugar until smooth, then slowly add eggs and bananas, mixing just until blended. In a small bowl, combine the remaining ingredients, stirring with a fork to mix, then add all at once to the banana mixture. Mix just until batter is blended-do not over beat! Spoon batter into prepared pans and bake 55- 60 minutes, or until wooden pick inserted in center comes out clean. Cool loaves in pan for 5 minutes, then turn onto wire rack to cool.

# Pineapple Bread

*This is my easy original recipe, and one that everyone loves!*

**INGREDIENTS:**
1-1/4 cup butter, softened
1-1/2 cups sugar
3 large eggs, beaten
2- 8 ounce cans crushed pineapple
3 teaspoons baking soda, dissolved in 2 tablespoons water
6 cups flour
3 teaspoons salt

**DIRECTIONS:**
Preheat oven to 350 F. Lightly grease three 8 x 4 inch loaf pans.

In a large mixing bowl, cream the butter and sugar until light, then add the eggs slowly, mixing just until blended. Stir in the pineapple with juice. Mix together the baking soda, flour and salt and stir into the batter just until mixed. Divide batter among the three pans and bake at 350 for 30 minutes, or until wooden pick inserted in center comes out clean.

# The Soup Kettle

At the Club, I always had at least one soup on the menu every night. Guests enjoyed this first course and looked forward to soup as part of the dinner meal. Today, this nice custom isn't as common at restaurants and it seems that you always have to ask if there is a Soup of the Day!

# Fish Broth (Stock)

*Many soup and chowder recipes start with fish broth instead of water. It makes a richer soup. Making fish broth is easy, unless you are afraid of working with a whole fish. Fish stock is just the fish parts (not the meat—the bones, head, tail) boiled with the seasonings of your choice. You can also add a cup of wine. Here is a simple recipe, and you can use all the seasonings or only ones you want.*

## INGREDIENTS:
2 pounds fish parts (bones, head, and tail)
2 quarts water
1 large onion, sliced
1 medium carrot, sliced
1 stalk celery
1 teaspoon ground black pepper
1 teaspoon salt
Juice of one lime
1 cup white wine
6 sprigs parsley
1 teaspoon thyme
1 bay leaf

## DIRECTIONS:
Wash the fish pieces in water and lime. Combine all ingredients in a large pot or Dutch oven and bring to a boil. Reduce heat to medium low and cover; simmer for 45 minutes to an hour. Remove pot from heat, strain broth well to remove all solids. Discard solids and set broth aside. Makes 2 quarts. If not using immediately, store in refrigerator.

# Fish Chowder

*Guests loved my fish soup, or chowder as many called it, and often asked why mine tasted so good. I always used fresh local fish and cleaned it well, and that makes all the difference in the world. If you can't make fresh coconut milk, you can substitute canned. This is a large recipe that serves 8.*

### INGREDIENTS:
2 pounds fresh grouper, snapper or dolphin, skinned, boned and cut into 1 inch pieces
Lime juice
3 tablespoons butter
1 large onion, chopped (1-1/2 cups)
1/2 cup diced celery
1 small green sweet pepper, chopped
4 cups fish broth
1 bay leaf
1 teaspoon salt
1 teaspoon black pepper
1 cup peeled and diced carrots
1-1/2 cups diced peeled Irish potatoes
2 cups coconut milk (fresh if possible)

2 tablespoons flour
¼ cup water
Paprika

### DIRECTIONS:
Wash the fish in cold water and lime, then dice into ½ inch pieces. Be sure to remove the bloodline and check carefully for any small bones or skin and remove them too.

In large stock pot or Dutch Oven, melt the butter and sauté the onions, celery and sweet pepper for 2-3 minutes over medium heat, stirring frequently, until turning soft. Add the fish broth, bay leaf and salt and pepper, stir well, then bring soup to a boil, stirring frequently. Stir in the remaining vegetables, reduce heat to medium, cover and cook 10 minutes. Add the coconut milk and cubed fish and return to a low boil, then simmer 10 minutes longer, or until fish is cooked. If you want thicker chowder, mix flour and water to form a smooth paste, then slowly stir into chowder and cook 8-10 minutes longer, until it thickens. Taste and adjust salt and pepper if desired. Add a sprinkling of paprika on top of each serving.

# Lobster Bisque

*This is a very popular old recipe that visitors to the islands always seemed to expect on the menu once they found out about all the lobsters we used to have here in Cayman. But it isn't a traditional Cayman dish. It makes a delicious first course, or luncheon dish, but does not keep well and should be served right away in heated bowls or cups, or it may thicken and become distasteful. This recipe serves 6 and can be doubled. Don't try to make this if you're in a rush.*

### INGREDIENTS:

2 medium Cayman whole lobsters
(with 8-inch tails)
2-1/2 cups water from boiled lobsters
1 medium onion, diced
1 large carrot, peeled and diced
1 large Irish potato, peeled and diced
4 medium ribs celery with leaves, chopped
2 whole cloves
1 small bay leaf, crushed
1 teaspoon salt

¼ teaspoon nutmeg
4 tablespoons butter
4 tablespoons flour
3 cups whole milk
1 tablespoon tomato
(optional)
1 cup light cream
Paprika
Sherry
1/2 teaspoon ground
black pepper

### DIRECTIONS:

Wash the lobsters in cold water first to clean off any sand or dirt. Boil in 1-1/2 quarts water, just until shells turn red, about 15 minutes. Remove lobsters from water and cool them until you can handle. Save the cooking water. Crack the shells and remove tail, leg and head meat, saving the shell pieces. Pick the meat over thoroughly to remove any pieces of shell, then dice the meat fine. Set aside.

Make the broth: crush the saved lobster shells and add to the measured lobster water in a large saucepan. Add the vegetables, cloves, bay leaf, salt, pepper and nutmeg and bring to a boil, stirring well. Reduce heat to a simmer and cook for 30 minutes. Remove from heat and strain broth well, using a fine sieve, discarding shells and solids. Set broth aside.

In clean saucepan, melt the butter over low heat and stir in the flour until smooth. Cook for one minute, stirring frequently, then slowly add the milk, using a wire whisk, blending until mixture is smooth. Stir in reserved broth, mixing until smooth, then add lobster meat and tomato paste. Stir well and bring to a low simmer-do not boil! Cover and simmer for five minutes, then remove from heat and stir in cream until smooth. Taste and adjust salt and pepper. Serve promptly in heated bowls and sprinkle lightly with paprika. Offer sherry to guests-some may not want it, others can add a tablespoon or a little more to suit their taste.

# Short Cut Lobster Bisque

*When I cooked for guests at the Club, I always made my dishes from scratch. But later when the world got so rushed and busy, I learned recipes like this one, that make life easier for people who don't have so much time to cook today.*

## INGREDIENTS:

1 can condensed mushroom soup
1 can condensed tomato bisque or tomato soup
1-1/2 - 2 cups milk
¼ teaspoon nutmeg
1 tablespoon minced onion or 1 teaspoon onion powder
1 teaspoon Worcestershire sauce
1 tablespoon sherry (more to taste)
½ teaspoon black pepper
1 cup diced cooked lobster meat
Paprika

## DIRECTIONS:

Combine soups and amount of milk for desired thickness in medium saucepan and blend well, then stir in remaining ingredients except lobster meat. Bring to a boil, then reduce heat to a simmer and stir well again. Simmer five minutes, stirring several times, then stir in lobster meat and cook until soup is heated through. Serve right away, sprinkled with paprika. Offer more sherry to guests to use as desired.

# Turtle Soup

*Of all my soups, this was the recipe guests asked for again and again. Turtle steak gives up juices with such a rich, delicious flavor that there is no substitute for it. Because of the laws today, we can't export farmed turtle meat anymore, so you won't be able to make this recipe at home unless you live here in Cayman.*

### INGREDIENTS:
3 pounds turtle steak, cut into small pieces
8 cups water
2 bay leaves
2 pounds Irish potatoes, peeled and diced
1 pound carrots, peeled and diced
1 cup chopped onions
1 cup whole canned tomatoes, crushed
Salt and pepper to taste
3 tablespoons flour
2 tablespoons water

### DIRECTIONS:
In a large saucepan or Dutch Oven, combine the turtle meat, water and bay leaves and stir well. Bring to rolling boil and then reduce heat to a low boil and cook 30 minutes. Add the vegetables, stir well and simmer until vegetables are tender. Add salt and pepper to taste, then dissolve flour in remaining water to make smooth paste and stir into soup-the flour gives it a "boost." Makes 8 servings.

# Conch Soup

*This recipe is from Honduras and was given to me by nephew Lin McLaughlin. It is more like a stew and very filling and delicious! As always, you must pound the conchs before you boil them so they are tender. (There are recipes for conch chowder in Cleo's Conch Recipes.)*

### INGREDIENTS:
4 cups diced cooked conch meat
2 -13.5 ounce cans coconut milk
6 cups water
½ pound sweet potatoes (West Indian kind, not American), peeled and diced
2 large slices breadfruit, peeled and diced
2 cups fresh diced tomatoes
½ pound carrots, sliced
½ cup chopped onion
2 green bananas, sliced
1 sprig thyme
Salt and black pepper to taste

### DIRECTIONS:
Combine all ingredients in a large pot or Dutch Oven and bring to a boil. Reduce heat and simmer for 20 minutes or longer, until vegetables are tender and soup is desired thickness. Remove thyme and salt and pepper to taste. Makes 8 very hearty servings.

# Coconut Soup

*This really should be done with freshly made coconut milk, but you can use canned coconut milk too. You can use more curry powder to taste, for a spicier soup, but I was conservative, considerate of the tastes of my foreign guests. It can be served chilled too.*

### INGREDIENTS:
1 tablespoon butter
2 tablespoons curry powder
3 cups fresh coconut milk
4-1/2 cups evaporated milk
4 chicken bouillon cubes or equivalent measure of chicken stock base
Fresh grated coconut (toasted if desired)

### DIRECTIONS:
In a large saucepan, melt the butter over medium heat and sprinkle over the curry powder. Stir well and cook for a minute, then add the coconut milk and evaporated milk and stir well, Add chicken cubes or base and stir well. Reduce heat to low and heat slowly, stirring frequently, until chicken cubes are dissolved and soup is heated through. Ladle into small bowls and serve with a sprinkling of fresh grated coconut on top, if desired. (To toast coconut, spread about ¼ cup fresh grated coconut on an ungreased baking sheet and bake at 350F for 10 minutes until light golden brown.) Serves 6.

# Vichyssoise a la Cleo

*I know that today most recipes call for leeks in this soup, but when I was cooking they were hard to come by and no one ever seemed to miss them. This is my recipe and good when you need a cool dish in the summer. Makes 8-12 servings.*

### INGREDIENTS:
½ cup butter
4 cups chopped yellow onion
4 cups water
4 teaspoons chicken bouillon granules or ¼ cup chicken base
1/2 cup instant mashed potatoes
4 cups evaporated milk or half and half
1 teaspoon salt
1 teaspoon ground white pepper
½ cup cooking sherry
1 tablespoon chopped parsley
Chopped scallions

## DIRECTIONS:

In large stockpot, melt butter and sauté onions until turning soft. Stir in water, bouillon or chicken base and bring to a boil. Cook for 2 minutes, stirring several times, then reduce heat to medium and stir in mashed potatoes. Stir until soup thickens and potatoes are dissolved, then add evaporated milk or half and half, salt and pepper, stirring well. Remove from heat and cool for 10 minutes. Puree the soup in a blender or food processor until smooth. Stir in the sherry and parsley and adjust salt and pepper if desired. Chill until cold. Serve in chilled bowls, garnished with chopped scallions if desired.

# Cleo's Prize Gazpacho

*I never thought I could win a contest for a dish like this. But one day a hotel guest from California wanted to see whose recipe for Gazpacho was better and I accepted his challenge. We let other guests be the judges and they liked my recipe much better than his! And I thought California was the home of cold soups like this! Long before it became common in Cayman, people were surprised to find this cold Spanish soup on my dinner menu. Be sure to make the soup at least four hours before serving so it has time to chill thoroughly.*

### INGREDIENTS:
1 large can tomato or V-8 juice (46 oz.)
   (1qt 14 oz size)
2 cups beef broth
1-1/2 cups finely chopped green peppers
1 medium ripe tomato, chopped
¾ cup finely chopped red or sweet onions
1 tablespoon olive oil or vegetable oil
1 tablespoon paprika

1 clove garlic, minced fine
1 teaspoon salt
1/8 teaspoon black pepper

### GARNISH:
Croutons
Chopped scallions (green onions)
Diced ripe avocado
Chopped onions

### DIRECTIONS:

Combine all ingredients except garnishes in a large plastic or glass container and mix well. Cover and chill four hours or longer. Ladle into 8 individual bowls and top with 1 teaspoon each of the garnishes. You can add a little Cayman pepper sauce to taste or offer it to guests on the side.

# Cleo's Cheese Soup

*This is a very rich dish, and can be served as a main course with a salad and fresh baked bread. Canadians who visited the Club brought me this recipe. They said it should be made only with real Canadian cheddar cheese—but that wasn't something you found in Cayman back then. Other people said it should have a pinch of nutmeg or Coleman's (dry) mustard or Worcestershire sauce—or more pepper. You can add whatever you want, including minced country pepper or Pickapeppa Sauce, but I didn't season my food too highly.*

## INGREDIENTS:

1 cup butter
1 pound carrots, grated
3 cups cheddar cheese, grated or shredded
3/4 cup flour
6 cups chicken broth
6 cups evaporated milk
3 pints beer
Parsley and additional Paprika

## DIRECTIONS:

In a large (5 quart) heavy saucepan or Dutch oven, melt the butter over medium heat and add the carrots. Cook, stirring frequently, until they turn soft --do not allow to brown. Reduce heat to medium-low, sprinkle with the cheese and stir to blend ingredients. Cook until cheese melts, being careful not to brown it, then stir in flour and mix well. Gradually stir in the broth and cream until smooth and cook, stirring constantly, until soup thickens. Slowly stir in the beer and blend well. Reduce heat to low and cook just until soup is hot. Do not allow soup to boil because if it gets too hot, the cheese will break down and soup may curdle. Ladle into cups with sprinkling of paprika on top for color. This recipe makes 30 small servings and can easily be halved. As with any recipe, you can vary the seasonings to suit your taste.

# French Onion Soup

*This was always a favorite on the menu. My secret to this easy recipe is cooking the onion slowly until it is almost caramelized—this gives the soup a much richer flavor. You can substitute chicken broth for beef broth and white wine for red wine or sherry for a lighter flavor.*

## INGREDIENTS:

¼ cup butter or margarine
2 tablespoons vegetable oil
6 large white onions, thinly sliced

1 teaspoon sugar
1/2 teaspoon freshly ground black pepper
1 teaspoon salt
1 cup dry red wine or port sherry
5 cups beef broth
1 sprig fresh thyme or 1 teaspoon dried
2 teaspoons Worcestershire sauce
6 slices French bread, toasted
½ cup grated parmesan cheese

**DIRECTIONS:**

Heat butter and oil in a Dutch oven over medium-high heat. Add onions to pan; sauté for 5 -8 minutes or until almost tender, stirring frequently. Reduce heat to medium; sprinkle onions with sugar, pepper and salt and cook, stirring frequently, until onion is turning golden brown (almost caramelized.) Stir in wine or sherry, broth, thyme and Worcestershire sauce; bring to a boil, stirring well. Reduce heat to low and simmer, covered, 30-45 minutes.

Preheat broiler. Place 6 ovenproof bowls on a jelly-roll pan. Ladle soup into each bowl. Top each bowl with slice of bread; sprinkle top generously with parmesan cheese. Broil 1-2 minutes or until cheese begins to brown. Makes 6 servings.

# Cream of Onion Soup

*You can use Vidalia or other sweet onions that are easy to find today for this recipe.*

**INGREDIENTS:**
2/3 cup butter
2 cups thinly sliced onion
¼ cup flour
1-1/2 teaspoons salt
¼ teaspoon pepper
1 quart whole milk

**DIRECTIONS:**

In a large saucepan, melt butter over low heat and sauté onions, stirring several times, until tender, and just starting to turn golden, about 20-30 minutes. Blend in flour, salt and pepper and cook over medium heat, stirring constantly, two minutes longer—do not let flour brown. Gradually stir or whisk in milk until mixture is smooth. Bring to a boil, stirring constantly, then reduce heat and simmer until mixture is slightly thickened, about a minute longer. Remove from heat and stir well. Let rest five minutes, then serve. Makes 6 servings.

# Minted Pea Soup

*This is very nice dish which is served cold. If you don't have fresh mint, use 2 tablespoons mint jelly and blend it in after soup is pureed or strained.*

### INGREDIENTS:
1 pound green split peas
6 cups water
1 teaspoon salt
4 cups chicken broth
1 tablespoon minced onion
2 cloves garlic, minced
1 sprig fresh mint
1/2 teaspoon salt
½ teaspoon black pepper
1 teaspoon sugar
2-3 cups chilled evaporated milk or cream
Chopped mint or parsley

### DIRECTIONS:
Rinse the peas and pick over, then place peas, water and 1 teaspoon salt in large saucepan and bring to a boil for 3 minutes. Remove from heat and let stand for an hour, then drain well. Add chicken broth, onion, garlic and mint, remaining salt and pepper and bring to a boil. Stir well, then reduce heat to simmer and cover. Cook until peas are tender. Remove from heat and either puree soup in batches in a blender or mash and strain through fine sieve. Chill soup 8 hours or overnight, then stir in sugar and desired amount of cream until blended. Adjust seasonings to taste. Serve in chilled bowls and garnish with chopped mint or parsley. Makes 6 servings.

# Cleo's Cayman Country Soup

*This is another easy and delicious soup —made quickly from things you'll find in your own kitchen.*

### INGREDIENTS:
½ pound bacon, cooked until crisp
1 medium onion, chopped (1/2 cup)
2 - 15 ounce cans cream of mushroom soup
1 cup water

1 cup evaporated milk
1 -15 ounce can cream style corn
1 - 15 ounce can red kidney or black beans, drained
Salt and black pepper


### DIRECTIONS:

In a large saucepan or small Dutch oven, cook the bacon over medium high heat until crisp, then remove. Drain off all but 1 tablespoon of bacon fat. In remaining fat sauté onion over medium heat, stirring frequently, until soft but not browned. Add the mushroom soup and stir until blended, then add the water and evaporated milk and mix until all ingredients are blended. Stir in the corn and beans. Heat over medium low heat, just until bubbles form at the edge, stirring several times. Continue cooking, stirring several times, until heated through—do not bring to a boil. Add salt and black pepper to taste before serving. Makes 6 servings.


# Cho-Cho Soup

*Cho-chos are what we call the little green squashes others call christophenes. This recipe sounded exotic to visitors, but is easy to make and makes good use of these vegetables which are bland and taste something like cucumbers.*


### INGREDIENTS:
3 medium cho-chos
1 8 ounce can sweet green peas
4 cups chicken broth
2 cups water
½ cup chopped cooked ham
½ cub shredded cabbage
Salt and pepper to taste


### DIRECTIONS:

Peel and dice the cho-chos; drain the canned peas, then mash and set aside. In a medium saucepan, combine the diced cho-chos, broth, water, ham and cabbage and bring to a boil over medium high heat. Reduce heat to simmer and cook, stirring several times, until cho-cho is soft. Stir in the mashed peas and salt and pepper to taste, and cook until soup is heated through. Makes 6 servings.

# Avocado Soup

*Caymanians love avocados, which we call "pears." The favorite way to eat them is to scoop the flesh from a very ripe soft pear and spread it on bread like butter. Years ago, pears were a very special treat and you had to go to George Town to get them. And today, after Hurricane Ivan destroyed so many trees, they are almost as scarce as they were a long time ago. I believe this recipe may be from Mexico or South America, and it is delicious on a hot summer day. The pears should be ripe, but over ripe and black.*

### INGREDIENTS:
3 cups chicken broth
2 medium Irish potatoes, peeled and diced
6 large scallions chopped, or 2 leeks, white part only, sliced thin
1 cup evaporated milk or cream
2 large ripe avocados peeled and diced
½ teaspoon salt
1/4 teaspoon pepper
Minced scallion or chives

### DIRECTIONS:
In medium saucepan, heat the chicken broth and add the scallion or leeks and potatoes and bring to a boil. (If using scallions, use only the white and palest green parts and save the green ends for garnish.) Reduce heat and simmer until vegetables are soft, about 20 minutes. Remove from heat and cool, then puree in a blender or food processor. Return mixture to saucepan and stir in the cream and heat through but do not allow to boil. Puree the avocado in blender or food processor and stir into cream mixture, blending until smooth. Add salt and pepper and adjust if necessary to suit your taste. Pour soup into a large bowl and cover, then refrigerate until cold. Serve with a sprinkling of minced scallion or chives on top as a garnish. Makes about 6 servings.

# Tasty Side Dishes

Packaged macaroni and cheese mix dates back to the 1940s and was one of the first "convenience foods" to become popular in Cayman. When I first took over the kitchen at Tortuga Club, I made this dish from scratch, but later used the Kraft packaged mix as a base. Macaroni and cheese was an exception to my rule of not using any packaged mixes in my kitchen. This recipe makes enough for a party-but it may be just enough for your household once they taste my recipe and demand seconds!

# Cleo's Custardy
# Macaroni & Cheese

*Cayman people have always been of two minds about this dish. Some like it firm enough to cut it with a knife. Others say it must be rich and custardy and spooned out of the baking dish-- which is how I always made mine and guests at the Club loved it! People still say I make the best macaroni and cheese. My secret is using "cream" or evaporated milk, a little fresh onion and real cheddar cheese on top. This gives it a much richer texture and flavor. I still make it today for church functions.*

### INGREDIENTS:
6 - 7.5 ounce boxes Kraft macaroni and cheese
3 tablespoons grated or minced onion
3 -14.5 ounce cans evaporated milk
1 cup (2 sticks) butter, cut into small pieces
3 cups shredded or grated cheddar cheese
Paprika

### DIRECTIONS:
Preheat oven to 350F. Lightly butter a steam table size pan (12 x 21 inch baking dish). Cook the macaroni until just turning tender-al dente. Do not allow to become soft. Drain macaroni well and pour into a large mixing bowl. While still hot, sprinkle with the cheese mix that comes with the package and the butter pieces and stir gently until butter is melted. Add the evaporated milk and grated onion and mix well. Spoon mixture into prepared pan and top with the cheddar cheese and a sprinkling of paprika for color. Bake for 30 minutes or until mixture is bubbling and top is golden brown. This recipe makes about 12 servings.

# Breadfruit Salad

*Caymanians love this dish-but Ivan took away so many of our breadfruit trees that this is now almost a luxury today. Guests used to say it was better than any potato salad they had ever eaten! Canned beets and mixed vegetables are typical Caymanian additions to breadfruit and potato salad.*

**INGREDIENTS:**
1 medium ripe breadfruit (about 4 cups)
½ cup chopped onion
1 cup celery, diced
½ cup red onion, minced
¼ cup chopped sweet green pepper
2 large hard-boiled eggs, peeled
and chopped

1 teaspoon salt or Nature's Seasons seasoning
1 teaspoon black pepper
1 - 8 ounce can mixed vegetables, well drained
1 - 8 ounce can diced beets, well drained
2 teaspoons lime juice
Mayonnaise or Miracle Whip salad dressing to taste.

**DIRECTIONS:**
Cook the breadfruit first. Peel and core the breadfruit and cut into slices. Boil in salted water with a half cup chopped onion until breadfruit is just turning soft-do not allow it to become mushy. Drain and discard onion. When cool enough to handle, cut breadfruit into bite-sized cubes and place in a large bowl. While still warm, add the celery, remaining onion, sweet pepper, eggs and seasonings and mix well, then fold in the canned beets and mixed vegetables and lime juice. Add enough mayonnaise or salad dressing to moisten the ingredients to your taste. Adjust the amount of salt and pepper as desired. Chill for at least an hour. Serves 8.

# Breadfruit Scallops

*I would surprise guests by serving this instead of scallop potatoes. Once they tried this, they never wanted potatoes again. You don't cook the breadfruit ahead of time for this recipe. This makes enough for 8 people.*

## INGREDIENTS:

6 pounds breadfruit (one large) peeled and slice thin
1 cup flour
½ teaspoon salt
½ teaspoon pepper
½ cup onions, chopped
½ cup margarine, cut into small pieces
2 cups cream (evaporated milk)
2 cups water
2 cups grated cheddar cheese

## DIRECTIONS:

Preheat oven to 400F. Grease or lightly butter a large (3 quart baking dish). In a medium bowl, combine the flour, onions, salt and pepper and toss to mix. Place a layer of breadfruit slices over the bottom of pan and sprinkle with a third of the flour mixture and a half of the margarine pieces. Repeat twice and end with the last of the flour mixture. Combine the cream and water and pour over breadfruit. Sprinkle top with cheese. Bake at 400 until breadfruit is tender and cheese is lightly browned-be careful and don't allow this to dry out. You can make it in a baking pan too, but a glass baking dish keeps the flavor nice.

# Corn Pudding and Corn Custard

These are not traditional Caymanian dishes, but recipes from the American South that I learned years ago. There were never any leftovers! I would serve them on the same menu with ham or fried chicken. As a young girl, I don't remember having corn that you could eat off the cob. No, no, it was too hard. We grew some corn, called guinea or broom corn, but my mother would shuck the corn, then hang it from the rafters to dry in the kitchen and then it had to be soaked and grated before you could use it. Most of the corn was grated used for porridge or heavy cake. Today I do like grits and wish I had known about them back then, as we threw out that part, the corn "trash", to the chickens!

Frozen and fresh corn are available at our supermarkets today and both make better dishes than canned corn. But I've kept these recipes as I did them at the Club.

# Corn Custard

*If you want to add a little Cayman touch, try a pinch of minced seasoning pepper or dash of Scotch Bonnet pepper sauce.*

## INGREDIENTS:
2 cups whole kernel canned corn, well drained
2 tablespoons sugar
1 teaspoon salt
2 tablespoons flour
1/2 teaspoon nutmeg
Pinch of red (cayenne) pepper or few drops pepper sauce
2 cups evaporated milk
3 large eggs, beaten
2 tablespoons butter, melted

## DIRECTIONS:
Preheat oven to 350 F. Lightly butter an 8 inch square (1-1/2 quart) baking dish. Place the corn in a medium mixing bowl, then sprinkle over it the sugar, salt, flour, nutmeg and pepper. In separate bowl combine the milk and eggs and stir into the corn mixture. Mix in the melted butter and spoon custard into prepared baking dish. Set the baking dish in a larger roasting pan and fill with hot water to halfway up the side of the baking dish. Bake for 45 minutes, until golden and set. A knife inserted in center should come out clean. This should not be over baked until it is too dark and firm. This recipe makes 6 to 8 servings.

# Corn Pudding

*This is firmer custard casserole than the corn custard. It is very good served with ham or fried chicken.*

**INGREDIENTS:**
4 large eggs, lightly beaten
2 cups evaporated milk
2 tablespoons butter, melted
1 tablespoon sugar
1-1/2 teaspoons salt
½ teaspoon black pepper
Pinch of red (cayenne) pepper or pepper sauce if desired
½ teaspoon nutmeg
1/2 cup homemade breadcrumbs or cracker crumbs
2 cups creamed-style corn
2 cups well drained whole kernel corn (canned, thawed frozen or fresh)

**DIRECTIONS:**
Preheat oven to 350F. Lightly butter a 9 x 13 inch square baking dish. In large mixing bowl, combine the eggs, milk and butter, and blend well, then add sugar, salt, pepper and spices and breadcrumbs and mix until smooth. Stir in the corn and spoon mixture into prepared baking dish. Set the dish in a larger roasting pan and pour hot water into pan to reach halfway up the baking dish. Bake 50-60 minutes, until top is golden brown and knife inserted in center comes out clean. *Makes 10 -12 servings*

# Scalloped Corn with Sweet Peppers

INGREDIENTS:
1 - 14-3/4 ounce can whole kernel corn
½ cup evaporated milk
2 tablespoons flour
1 teaspoon salt
¼ teaspoon black pepper
1 teaspoon celery salt
2 large eggs, beaten
3 tablespoons chopped sweet green pepper
2 tablespoons chopped pimento
¼ cup buttered breadcrumbs *

DIRECTIONS:
Preheat oven to 350 F. Lightly butter an 8-inch square baking dish. Drain the corn well, reserving liquid in a 1-cup measuring cup. Add enough of the evaporated milk to measure a full cup of liquid. Melt butter in a large saucepan over medium heat until bubbling, then stir in the flour, salt, pepper and celery salt, blending until smooth. Cook one minute, then stir in the liquid mixture and cook, stirring constantly, until mixture thickens, about two minutes. Stir a few tablespoonfuls of this mixture into the beaten eggs, then stir this back into the sauce, reduce heat to low and cook until smooth, about three minutes longer. Stir in the corn, sweet peppers and pimento and pour into baking dish. Sprinkle top with breadcrumbs. Place baking dish in larger pan and fill with hot water reaching halfway up the baking dish. Bake 45 -50 minutes until top is golden. Makes about 6 servings.

*(To make buttered breadcrumbs, place ¼ cup breadcrumbs in a small bowl and sprinkle with 1 teaspoon melted butter. Toss with a fork.)

# Beets in Orange Sauce
## (Royal Beets)

*This is an old recipe from the southern US.*

**INGREDIENTS:**
¼ cup brown sugar
1 teaspoon cornstarch
1 tablespoon butter
¾ cup orange juice
1 tablespoon lime juice
½ teaspoon salt
½ teaspoon black pepper or to taste
1-16 ounce can sliced beets, well drained

**DIRECTIONS:**
In small bowl, whisk together the sugar and cornstarch. In a medium saucepan, melt the butter over medium heat and stir in the sugar mixture, mixing until blended. Reduce heat to medium low and slowly stir in the orange and lime juices, salt and pepper. Cook until mixture thickens, then gently stir in the beets, being careful not to mash them. Heat through and serve hot. This goes well with pork or chicken.

# Cleo's Conch Recipes

When foreign guests saw a live conch for the first time in the shell, they would be shocked that this was the same thing I cooked for them. They would ask me: "Miss Cleo, how did you ever learn how to eat those things?" Well, I don't know how people first learned you could eat conchs, but conch was what we were raised on in East End and fed us many days. Lots of people in Cayman still say that you have to come to East End to eat the best conch dishes.

My family loved stew conch with coconut milk. Sometimes our supper was even simpler: conch pounded, boiled and eaten with fresh lime. In those days, conchs were big and sweet and so plentiful in East End! You just walked off the beach at Colliers and they were thick in the shallow water all around. The conch we ate was always so fresh. Not like today. Most conch in Cayman is imported now, and some are sold even though they are grey and dry and taste bad. I don't understand this.

It's best if you cook the conch first and then add to the stew. I would never grind my conchs, not even for chowders! Grinding conch makes it too fine and makes the chowder like pap (thin porridge.) After washing with limes and looking them over carefully to clean off any sand and grit, I would pound the conchs with a meat mallet until they looked almost like lace. Then I would boil them until tender and cut them into pieces. How big were the pieces? Well, that would depend on the dish. Stew conch needed bigger pieces to go with pie (sea pie). But conch chowder would be finely diced pieces.

Now when you boil conches, don't salt the water-this makes them tough. And you have to watch the pot and skim off the foam that rises to the top, because if it boils over onto the stove, it makes a mess. If the conchs are not fresh, the water helps remove the foulness and that's why it should be thrown out and not used in the recipe. Boil the conchs first, then make the recipe with fresh water or liquid such as chicken bouillon.

You can pressure (cook) the conchs too, but they still have to be put in a big pot and boiled first. This works well for larger pieces especially. Remove the conchs from the pot after boiling and put in a pressure cooker a quarter full of water and pressure for 25 -30 minutes.

## Tips for cooking conch:

- Of course you don't cook the conchs in the shell, no matter what anyone tells you.
- Conch should be fresh, cleaned and well tenderized before using in recipes.
- You should have plenty of lime handy to freshen and wash the conchs and to clean you hands and knives and other utensils. There is nothing better!
- You need to pound conchs even if they are to be cooked in a pressure cooker, as the muscle will be tough otherwise.
- Be sure to watch the pot carefully when boiling conch, and skim off the foam that will rise or it will boil over and make a smelly mess on the stove.
- Throw away the boiling water and use fresh water for your recipe-or the cooking water will turn your recipe off color, even blue.

# Old Time East End Stew Conch

*In the old days, our stew conch was just conch pounded, cut up and boiled, then cooked slowly, over a low fire, in freshly made coconut milk and whatever seasoning was on hand. Sometimes we would find an onion on the beach, washed in from a passing ship, and that made it even better. It is the slow cooking that makes stew conch so good. The coconut milk cooks down and thickens and the sweetness of the coconut and the conch make a rich, delicious and simple meal!*

*Later some people began to use pressure cookers to make stew conch-but you still have to pound the conch and cut it up, and boil it first or it will not be tender! And it is always important to add a little ground black pepper to give it a boost.*

### INGREDIENTS:
2 dozen large conch, cleaned
3 dry coconuts
20 cups water, divided
1 cup sliced onions
1 medium sweet green pepper, sliced
1 whole orange or yellow Scotch Bonnet or Mutton pepper
Salt and ground black pepper to taste

### SEA PIE:
3 cups flour
½ teaspoon salt
Water
Additional flour for board

**DIRECTIONS:**

Pound conchs thoroughly with a meat mallet until tenderized. Place conchs in a large stock pot or Dutch oven with 12 cups (3 quarts) of water and bring to a boil. Skim off any foam that rises and reduce heat to simmer. Cook conchs until tender, about an hour. Drain conchs and dice into small pieces. Set aside.

While conchs are boiling, make the coconut milk. Remove the white meat from the coconuts and cut in small pieces. In batches, place meat in blender or food processor with the remaining 8 cups of water and process until pureed and coconut is fine enough to squeeze the liquid from the "trash" or coconut solids. Strain coconut milk and discard trash. (We would feed this to the chickens.)

Pour the coconut milk into a large stockpot and bring to a boil. Reduce heat and keep at a medium boil until oil begins to appear on the surface, about 30 minutes. Add 3 more cups of water, stir well, and add the conch, sweet pepper and onion. Stir well.

Add one whole orange or yellow Cayman pepper (Scotch Bonnet), being careful not to pierce it, to coconut milk with boiled conch and other ingredients. Return to a boil, then reduce heat to low and simmer until liquid has cooked down almost to desired thickness. The last and most important thing is to make sea pie-no Cayman stew conch is complete with this.

**To make sea pie:**

In a large bowl, combine the flour and salt and slowly stir in enough water to form soft dough which will be a little lumpy, but firm enough to handle. Knead gently until it comes together and you can stretch it. Place on lightly floured board and roll out with a rolling pin until very thin. Let the dough rest for 20 minutes after rolling. Cut into strips, and then into 1 -1/2 inch strips about 1 inch wide and lay sea pie pieces on top of simmering stew. Cook until firm but not tough, about 20 minutes. Add salt and black pepper to taste to stew before serving. Makes 16-20 servings.

## How Sea Pie got its name:

No one really knows how this essential ingredient of Cayman stew conch got its name. Sea Pie is simple flat "noodles that aren't noodles." There is an art to making this very simple traditional Caymanian ingredient, however. They are supposed to be light and tender, not chewy. Cleo insists the real name is SEE Pie, because the dough has to be almost transparent- -"thin enough to spy through" or see through, before cutting into pieces and adding to the stew. Sounds easy doesn't it? There's one more ingredient missing from this recipe: patience. It takes more than a pinch of that when handling the dough to make proper sea pie!

# Cleo's Prize Conch Stew

*I am proud of this recipe, which won top honors in the 1991 Caribbean Culinary Salon. It was one of the first Caribbean cooking competitions, organized by the Caribbean Hotel Association. My unusual combination of tomato paste and coconut milk is a delicious change from traditional Cayman coconut conch stew.*

### INGREDIENTS:
2 dozen large conch, cleaned
3 coconuts
20 cups water, divided
1 bay leaf
½ teaspoon thyme
1 cup sliced onions
1 medium sweet green pepper, sliced
1 can tomato paste (6 ounces)
Salt and ground black pepper to taste

### SEA PIE:
3 cups flour
½ teaspoon salt
Water
Additional flour for board

### DIRECTIONS:
Pound conchs thoroughly with a meat mallet until tenderized. Place conchs in a large stock pot or Dutch oven with 12 cups (3 quarts) of water and bring to a boil. Skim off any foam that rises and reduce heat to simmer. Cook conchs until tender, about an hour. Drain conchs and dice into small pieces. Set aside.

While conchs are boiling, make the coconut milk. Remove the white meat from the coconuts and cut in small pieces. In batches, place meat in blender or food processor with the remaining 8 cups of water and process until pureed and coconut is fine enough to squeeze the liquid from the "trash." Strain coconut milk and discard trash.

Pour the coconut milk into a large stockpot and bring to a boil. Reduce heat and keep at a medium boil until oil begins to appear on the surface, about 30 minutes. Add 3 more cups of water, stir well, and the conch, bay leaf, thyme, sweet pepper, onion and tomato paste, stir well, then reduce heat to simmer until liquid has cooked down and thickened. Add the sea pie.

**To make sea pie:**

In a large bowl, combine the flour and salt and slowly stir in enough water to form soft dough which will be a little lumpy, but firm enough to handle. Knead gently until it comes together and you can stretch it. Place on lightly floured board and roll out with a rolling pin until very thin. Let rest for 20 minutes after rolling. Cut into strips, and then into 1 -1/2 inch strips about 1 inch wide and lay sea pie pieces on top of simmering stew. Cook until firm but not tough, about 20 minutes. Add salt and black pepper to taste to stew before serving. Makes 16-20 servings.

# Conch Steak

*My conch steak was so sweet and tender it would just melt in your mouth. I used only local conchs that were fresh from the sea and that made a big difference. And make your own breadcrumbs—don't use canned or seasoned ones from the store. Using cream (evaporated milk) gives a nicer flavor, but you can use whole milk too.*

**INGREDIENTS:**

6 large conchs, cleaned
3 cups homemade bread crumbs
¼ teaspoon salt
¼ teaspoon black pepper
1 cup cream (evaporated milk)
Vegetable oil

**DIRECTIONS:**

Pound the conchs well with a meat mallet and then place in large pot or Dutch oven with enough unsalted water to cover. Bring to a boil and skim off any foam, then reduce heat to low and simmer 25 minutes. Remove from water and pat dry. In a medium bowl, combine the breadcrumbs, salt and pepper. Pour the cream or milk into a shallow bowl. Dip each conch in cream, then into breadcrumbs, until thoroughly coated. In a large heavy skillet, add enough oil to cover the bottom and heat over medium high heat until hot. Add conch steaks, one at a time, but do not crowd pan. Fry until golden brown, about 3 minutes on each side. Add more oil as necessary to fry properly. Serve hot with tartar sauce. Makes 6 servings.

# Scallop Conchs

*Guests at Tortuga Club loved this dish and there were never any leftovers. This recipe is easy to make-but use fresh breadcrumbs, not dried ones from a can. As always, you can add more seasoning, like minced country pepper, if you want.*

**INGREDIENTS:**
4 -5 large conchs, cleaned
1 cup yellow onions, diced
1 cup chopped celery
1 cup chopped sweet (green) pepper
½ cup butter
3 cups soft breadcrumbs
1 teaspoon salt
1 teaspoon ground black pepper
3 cups evaporated milk
2 cups reserved water from conch

**INGREDIENTS:**
Pound the conchs thoroughly with a meat mallet and place in a pot of water. Bring to a boil and skim off the dirty foam. Then drain off and replace with fresh water. Return conchs to a boil and cook until tender. Reserve 2 cups of the cooking water. Cut conch into strips 2 inches long and ½ inch wide.

Preheat oven to 350 and butter a 9 x 13 inch baking dish. In a large skillet, melt the butter and cook the onion, celery and sweet pepper until turning soft. Remove from heat and sprinkle with breadcrumbs, salt and pepper and toss gently to combine-don't make mush. Place a layer of conch in the baking dish, then cover with a layer of the breadcrumb mixture. Repeat until all ingredients are used, ending with a top layer of breadcrumbs. Combine the milk and cooking water and pour over the top of conch mixture. Bake at 350 for 30 minutes, until set and golden on top. Remove from oven and let cool for five minutes, but serve hot!

# Conch Fritters

*Everyone loved my conch fritters! They were the most requested appetizer at the Club. My fritters were different from the ones you find everyplace else. Cooking the fritters in hot oil in a frying pan rather than deep oil, lets them cook evenly, and makes sure the fritters don't have soggy, uncooked centers. You can add more seasoning or a pinch of minced Cayman pepper to taste, but when I made these for guests, I had to be careful about that!*

### INGREDIENTS:
2 cups chopped, cooked conch (about 3 medium conchs)
1 cup flour
1 teaspoon baking powder
¼ teaspoon salt (seasoned salt may be used)
1/2 teaspoon ground black pepper
2 tablespoons finely chopped onion
2 tablespoons finely chopped green pepper
1 tablespoon vegetable oil
2/3 cup beer

**Additional vegetable oil for frying**

### DIRECTIONS:
First wash the conch in lime juice, then pound and tenderize with a mallet. Boil in unsalted water 20 minutes and cool, before chopping into small pieces. Otherwise the conch pieces will be too tough, even if chopped, to use in this recipe.

In a large mixing bowl, combine all ingredients and mix well. Pour ½ inch oil into a large heavy skillet or frying pan. Heat the oil until hot-350-375 F. but not smoking. Drop batter by tablespoons into skillet and flatten slightly into oblong shape instead of round balls-the fritter will cook better. Fry until golden brown, turning during cooking so they brown evenly. Remove from oil and drain on brown paper bag or other absorbent paper. Serve hot with tartar sauce or cocktail sauce or ketchup, if preferred. Makes about 2 dozen fritters.

# Conch Salad (Marinated Conch)

This was another popular appetizer that some guests liked so much they could have made it an entire meal. This is a very simple way to make marinated conch and good for a beach picnic when you have fresh caught conchs. You can add ketchup, Worcestershire sauce and Pickapeppa Sauce as desired to this recipe to make it spicier.

## INGREDIENTS:
4 large conchs, cleaned
1 small onion
1 stalk celery
1/2 small green pepper
1/2 cup fresh lime juice (more to taste)
1/2 cup cider vinegar
salt, black pepper & hot pepper sauce to taste

## DIRECTIONS:
Pound conch until very thin and well-tenderized, then cut into small pieces or very thin slices, using a sharp knife. Peel and dice onion, celery and sweet pepper into small pieces. Combine all ingredients except salt and pepper and mix well; refrigerate for an hour or more. Add salt, pepper and hot pepper sauce if desired to taste & mix well. Serve with Saltine crackers.

# Conch Chowder, East End Style

I always made my chowder with cream (evaporated milk) and not tomatoes and lots of conch. That's how people in East End like their conch chowder. I know the tomato kind is how they make it in the Bahamas, but here in Cayman, tomatoes and conch didn't come together until tourism started. And I always cooked the potatoes and added them at the end. Otherwise, the time it takes to make them tender would break down the soup. Also, I never used hot pepper when I cooked for guests but many people today like pepper in their chowder, so I have added it here.

## INGREDIENTS:
3 tablespoons butter, oil or bacon fat
6 tablespoons flour
1 teaspoon salt or to taste
1 teaspoon black pepper, or to taste
2 cups chicken broth
2 cups evaporated milk

1 cup diced onion
½ cup diced celery
*1/4 -1/2 teaspoon thyme
1 -2 tablespoons sherry
*Seasoning or country pepper slivers, if desired
6 cups (about 4 large) cooked tenderized conch, cut into small pieces
2 cups cooked potatoes, diced

### DIRECTIONS:

In a large saucepan or stockpot, melt the butter or heat the oil over medium heat. Sprinkle with the flour, salt and pepper and stir well to blend, then cook for one minute. Do not allow this mixture to brown. Stir in the chicken broth with a whisk, until smooth, then add the evaporated milk, onion and celery. Cook over medium heat, stirring frequently, until vegetables are soft and chowder has thickened.

Stir in the conch and potatoes and cook over low heat. Now, if you like more seasoning, add the thyme and sherry. You can also add a few slivers of Cayman hot pepper to suit your taste. Cook over low heat until chowder is very hot, but do not allow to boil. Adjust salt and pepper if needed. This will be thick and you can add more milk to suit your taste, but remember to adjust seasonings too.

## Thickening soups and sauces with flour

If you need to thicken a soup or stew, mix one part flour with two parts cold water or stock until a smooth paste forms. Usually a few tablespoons of flour will thicken a large pot. Stir mixture into the simmering soup or stew as needed, until desired thickness. You must cook the soup or stew for at least five minutes longer to remove the raw taste of the uncooked flour.

# Red Conch Chowder

*Red conch chowder is not a traditional Caymanian recipe. I learned to make this after I was at the Club awhile and it was very popular. Some say it reminded them of a clam chowder they knew at home, only much better! If you ask for conch chowder in Cayman today, the tomato kind is what you'll usually be served. You can serve each bowl with a little sherry on the side to be added right before eating.*

## INGREDIENTS:

1/4 pound bacon or salt pork
2 cups chopped yellow onion
1 cup chopped green pepper
3 cloves fresh garlic, chopped
1 cup diced carrots
¾ cup diced celery
8 large cleaned tenderized conch, cooked and cut into small pieces
2 15- ounce cans stewed tomatoes, undrained
4 cups water or fish broth
2 tablespoons tomato paste
1 bay leaf
1 teaspoon dried thyme
1 teaspoon Old Bay Seasoning
2 teaspoons ground black pepper to taste
1 teaspoon garlic salt
2 tablespoons Worcestershire sauce
1 whole Scotch Bonnet, unpierced
1-1/2 cups peeled diced Irish potatoes
Sherry

## DIRECTIONS:

Cut bacon into small pieces (or dice salt pork very fine) and cook over medium heat in a Dutch oven or heavy pot, stirring often, until the fat has almost cooked away and pork is browned but not crisp. Remove bacon or pork from pan and drain off all but 2 tablespoons of fat and add onions, garlic green pepper, carrots and celery. Cook over medium heat until vegetables are just beginning to soften, about 3 minutes.

Add the conch, tomatoes, broth, tomato paste and remaining ingredients except for potatoes. Be careful not to pierce the whole scotch bonnet or your chowder will be too hot! Bring to a boil and stir well. Reduce heat to medium low and simmer, stirring often, for about 45 minutes. Add the potatoes and cook until tender, about 20 minutes longer. Taste the chowder and add salt if necessary. Remove bay leaf and stir in the cooked bacon if desired. Pass the sherry so each guest can add a measure if desired. Makes 12 servings.

# Cayman Turtle

Sea turtles figure prominently in East End's history, especially the green sea turtle, Chelonia mydas. By the early 20th century turtle fishing was an important industry in Cayman. Caymanian built schooners sailed hundreds of miles in search of turtles, to Cuba, Honduras and the Miskito Cays off Nicaragua carrying seamen from East End, West Bay and George Town. East End was home not only to master shipwrights and turtle fishermen-but also some of the best turtle and seafood recipes in Cayman.

Turtle stew is still considered Cayman's national dish, relished by many today. But the turtle featured on local menus is farmed, not wild. It comes from breeding stock at the Cayman Turtle Farm Ltd. founded as Mariculture Ltd in 1968. Cayman's wild sea turtles, their nests and eggs have been protected by law since 1969, when the Turtle Protection Law came into effect. Those regulations later became part of Cayman's Marine Conservation Laws. Today only a few licensed Caymanian fishermen are allowed to continue the tradition of turtling out of respect for our heritage, and only between November 1 and April 30.

My turtle dishes were some of the most requested recipes at the Club. My recipes turned turtle steak into a tender delicacy that left clean plates from guests including HRH Prince Charles --and once, even a love note!

I learned from my father and mother how to cook turtle. Like most East End people, I used to enjoy it as a young girl. We especially loved turtle eggs, which we ate boiled. We just used to open them and eat the yolk with a little salt, and throw away the white part. Turtle eggs were always a delicacy. Some claimed they gave men a "boost" in their love life. We would also make corned turtle, soaking the meat in brine to preserve it. We would cook corned turtle in coconut milk, like rundown. You never hear about that today.

When I got older, I had to stop eating turtle because it made me feel weak. No one could ever explain why and this always puzzled the doctor. So I couldn't eat turtle anymore. But that didn't stop me from cooking it for others and watching them enjoy my recipes.

I knew that guests might not like the strong flavors and meat parts of Cayman turtle stew, but turtle steak cooked properly is tender and delicious. You must cook turtle steak slowly. It has to be browned first, then cooked with liquid and seasoning to make it tender and bring out the flavor. I see these chefs today just throw turtle steak on the grill or tossed in the pan with harsh spices and I shake my head. That's not the way you cook Cayman turtle. It needs to be cooked slowly…just like the turtle moves.

# Cleo's Prime Turtle Steak

*I never used tomatoes in my turtle steak or strong spices like tarragon or oregano as some do today. This is my recipe that I served at the Club. One afternoon I served my turtle steak to a very special guest, HRH Prince Charles who came for lunch at the club during a Royal Visit in the 1960s. He just loved this dish and didn't leave a scrap on his plate! I was very proud of that. My recipe was truly 'fit for royalty!'*

## INGREDIENTS:
10 -8 ounce Cayman Turtle Farm turtle steaks
2 cups flour
¼ cup vegetable oil
8 cups water
8 beef bouillon cubes
2 medium green peppers, sliced
2 medium onions, sliced
1 tablespoon Kitchen Bouquet
1/4 teaspoon thyme
2 bay leaves, crushed
2 teaspoons salt
2 golden Cayman (Scotch bonnet) peppers, seeded and cut into pieces
Salt and ground black pepper

## DIRECTIONS:
Pound the turtle steaks with a meat mallet or tenderizer until flattened to the size of your hand. Dredge each piece in flour until well coated, shaking off excess. In a Dutch oven or large heavy skillet, heat oil over medium high heat until hot and brown each steak on both sides. Cook turtle in batches, adding more oil if necessary-oil must be hot or meat will not brown properly. Remove steaks from pan as they are browned and drain on brown paper or paper towels.

**Make the gravy:** In the same pan, stir in the water and bouillon, loosening any browned bits sticking to the bottom. Over medium high heat, add the onions, sweet pepper and remaining ingredients and stir well, Bring to a boil, stirring several times, then add the turtle steaks. Cover pot tightly and reduce heat to low. Cook turtle slowly on low for 30 minutes, or until sauce has thickened and turtle is fork tender. Add more salt and black pepper to taste.

This is especially good served with homemade mashed potatoes and buttered fresh carrots, garnished with parsley sprigs. This makes 10 servings.

# Turtle Stroganoff

*Guests loved this dish and always asked for seconds. Homemade cream sauce, instead of sour cream, was the secret. I remember one night, a table of six sent back their plates, clean as can be, after a second helping. Stuck to the bottom of one plate was a handwritten note on a paper napkin. It said "This was delicious! We Love You, Miss Cleo!" You won't be able to make this at home because you can't find green turtle meat outside of Cayman today, but you can use beef or veal as a substitute. This recipe makes about 12 servings.*

**INGREDIENTS:**
¼ cup margarine
5 pounds turtle steak
Salt and black pepper to taste
2 teaspoons black pepper
1 cup sliced yellow onion
I cup sliced mushrooms
2 cups beef broth
3 cups water
1 teaspoon Kitchen Bouquet
¼ cup cooking sherry

5 cups rich cream sauce
1/4 cup sherry

**CREAM SAUCE:**
10 tablespoons margarine
10 tablespoons flour
5 cups cream (evaporated milk)
Salt and black pepper to taste

Cooked egg noodles

**DIRECTIONS:**

Wash the turtle meat in cold water and vinegar or lime juice and pat dry. Pound each steak with a meat mallet until flattened to the size of your hand. Slice into small (1 inch) pieces and sprinkle evenly with salt and pepper. Let rest 10 minutes.

In a 5 quart Dutch oven, melt the butter over medium high heat and add the turtle steak, a little at a time to keep the heat even, and stir frequently, until all the meat is browned well. Stir in the onions and mushrooms, cook until they just being to soften, then add the beef broth, water and Kitchen Bouquet. Stir well and bring to a boil, then reduce heat to medium low. Cook uncovered, stirring occasionally until meat is tender and the stock reduced by two thirds, about 45 minutes to an hour, depending on the meat. If the mixture starts to dry out, add another cup of water and stir well.

Make the cream sauce: In a large saucepan, melt the butter over medium low heat and using a wooden spoon, gradually add the flour, and cook for 2 minutes, stirring constantly, just until flour is cooked-do not brown! Gradually add the cream, stirring constantly, until mixture is smooth, then add the salt and pepper. Cook another five minutes, stirring frequently, until mixture thickens. Stir the cream sauce into the turtle meat and blend well, then add the sherry. Cook until mixture is heated through. Adjust salt and pepper to taste. Serve over hot egg noodles.

Adapting foreign recipes using local ingredients was one of Cleo's talents as Cayman's first female executive chef. France, Italy and Germany all have variations of veal birds, a classic rolled, stuffed meat dish. Her variation using turtle steak won raves from local and overseas guests.

# Turtle Birds

*I read about Veal Birds in a cookbook and thought I would make my own recipe using Cayman turtle steak instead. Guests laughed at the unusual name of this dish—and they always talked about it after. Many wrote to me asking for the recipe, but didn't realize that they couldn't find sea turtle meat back home.*

## INGREDIENTS:
4 turtle steaks
Salt and black pepper
1/2 pound bacon, finely chopped
1 cup fine dry bread crumbs
2 eggs, lightly beaten
½ teaspoon dried thyme
½ cup butter or margarine, melted
1 cup flour
Vegetable oil
2 cups evaporated milk or cream
½ teaspoon thyme

## DIRECTIONS:
Heat oven to 325 F. Line a 9 x 13 inch baking pan with foil or lightly grease. Cut meat into 8 serving pieces and pound with a meat mallet until 4 inches x 3 inches and about ¼ inch thick in size. Sprinkle each piece with salt and pepper on both sides. Fry the bacon pieces until most of the fat is rendered, then drain on paper towels.

Make the stuffing: in small bowl, combine bacon, bread crumbs, eggs, thyme and butter or margarine and mix well. Place a generous spoonful of stuffing mixture on each portion of turtle and roll up lengthwise, then fasten with toothpicks. Place flour in shallow bowl and roll each piece in flour and set aside on plate. In large heavy skillet, add enough oil to cover the bottom and heat over medium high heat until hot. Brown each turtle bird on all sides, then place in prepared pan. Combine cream and remaining thyme and pour evenly over turtle pieces, cover and bake for 1 hour at 325. Makes 8 servings.

# Turtle 911

I was driving Cleo home from George Town one steamy August afternoon in 2004, and she was chatting, filling me in mile by mile, on the latest neighborhood news from East End. That's when I heard the story about the Caymanian man who called 911 over a turtle.

As we passed into Gun Bay, she pointed at a house up a fairly steep hill on the north side of the road, a good distance from the sea.

"See that house up there? A big turtle crossed the road and crawled up into that man's yard the other night while he was sleeping. I hear that thing was very big!" Cleo said.

"Well it was late and very dark outside that night. He woke up and heard this commotion outside and looked out the window. There was this big black thing in his garden, right in the middle of his pumpkins! There was nothing he could do about something that big, so he picked up the phone and called 911! He said to the operator: "Come get this damn thing outta my yard!"

"That poor turtle! Well, someone did come and take it away. I guess they carried it back to the sea. But you know if it had been a green turtle and crawled up to the yard of one of those East End boys it would have been in the pot for sure!"

East End's beaches have been a nesting area for sea turtles for hundreds of years, but green turtles usually come ashore to lay their eggs in June and July. A turtle that large, nesting that late, would most likely have been a loggerhead. Loggerheads are seldom seen in the Cayman Islands and very rarely come ashore to lay their eggs. Adults of this species are slow, lumbering creatures about 4 feet long and weigh over 1000 pounds. They are the largest of the sea turtles but unlike the green and hawksbill turtles, not considered an edible delicacy.

An encounter with a giant sea turtle in the inky dark of a tropical night might be frightening. But just imagine the poor turtle's confusion! Whatever instinct compelled it to struggle all the way up the steep rocky incline from the sea, across a stretch of asphalt, and up a rugged hill is a mystery. But that's not as odd as someone calling 911 over a displaced reptile! Maybe that was a good thing. The poor turtle probably needed an ambulance with oxygen after that incredible journey.

--Barbara Currie Dailey

# Cleo's Wonderful Fish Recipes

Along with my pies and desserts, I was famous for my fish and seafood dishes. One night at the Club, the owner of a famous restaurant in George Town was a dinner guest. I served Snapper Meuniere. He told me it was the best fish he had ever eaten, done perfectly, and asked if I would come to his restaurant and "teach his chef how to cook fish like this." Well, I never did go, but if I had, I would have told that foreign chef the same thing I am telling you in these pages. You have to start with fresh fish and have a light hand cooking it.

I always bought most of our fish fresh from our local fishermen. Sometimes I did use imported fish and shellfish we could not buy here, like shrimp and sole. In days gone, here in East End, we knew the fishermen and they would bring fish right to the door of the kitchen. If you wanted fish to cook at home, if you couldn't get a whole ocean turbot, snapper or old wife you could always buy a piece of a big fish someone was cutting. But there are not as many fishermen now and most fish is sold whole to supermarkets or restaurants. It is hard to get fresh local fish in Cayman now.

Salmon and tilapia are popular today but they are farmed fish, not from the sea. When I was in the kitchen, these fish were not common in Cayman, and if we did get salmon, it was wild salmon and a special occasion. I won't even buy farmed salmon today because much of it has such a high scent and has artificial color added, so you can't tell how old it is. Tilapia is good, but it is a very mild fish and tastes like the seasoning you use on it.

# Cleo's Tips for Cooking Fish

• Learn how to tell fish is fresh and buy fresh fish whenever possible. It makes a big difference in any recipe. Fresh fish should not smell, except for a faint salty sweet scent like the sea. If the fish is whole, the eyes should be clean and clear, not cloudy or glazed. All flesh should be shiny and firm and not look dry, gray or pulling away from the bone.

• These same rules apply if you buy local fish from the boat. Make sure it was chilled properly after it was caught. Some of the fishermen today are not as careful as the old ones about keeping fish on ice in the boat. You have to be careful and know that locally caught "fresh" fish can be spoiled by the sun quickly.

• Wash the fish. The biggest problem I see today is people don't clean their fish properly before cooking. If you buy a whole fish that hasn't already been cleaned, clean it right away by removing the guts and scales first, then skin and bloodline. Wash the cleaned fish in cold water and lime juice or white vinegar to remove any foulness. This is very important. This rule is for fish filets and steaks too. Wash the pieces in cold water and lime juice even if they look clean. This will freshen the taste.

• Remove the skin and bloodline (the dark meat around the center bone). The skin and bloodlines are where any foulness will hide and taint the flavor of the fish. The exception to this is if you are baking a whole stuffed fish. Many leave the skin on to hold the fish together. But a better way is to filet the fish and bake the stuffing between the two pieces of fish.

• Look over every fish filet carefully to remove any bones! This is very important, especially when serving fish with a sauce or in a casserole where it would be hard to see any small pin bones.

• Do not let fish soak too long in lime juice or vinegar unless you are making fish ceviche. Longer than 20 minutes will begin to "cook" the fish and make it too soft.

• Do not overcook! No matter how you cook fish-- broiling, steaming, grilling or sautéing, fish should separate slightly when prodded with a knife, but not fall apart or it is overdone. You need to know your fish too: some fish like tuna and wahoo are dry and overcooking ruins them.

• Do not eat barracuda. This is hard to tell Caymanians, who love this fish, but it can be poison (with ciguatera.)There is no barracuda today that is safe for sure. And those tests with ants and coins are folk tales and don't work. You can't tell if a fish is poison until it's too late.

# Fish 'N Chips

*People still ask today when I am going to open my restaurant and make fish and chips again. On Friday nights, people drove from as far as George Town for this dish. The secret was my beer batter that cooked up light and crispy! And I served it hot from the fryer, with tartar sauce. A secret: make the beer batter right before using it.*

### FISH:
2 pounds cod, dolphin fish or other white fish fillets, cut into four ounce pieces
Salt and pepper
Flour
2 cups flour
3 teaspoons baking powder
½ teaspoons salt
1 12-ounce can beer

### CHIPS
1 1/2 pounds baking potatoes, cut into 1/2 inch slices
Vegetable oil
Salt to taste

### CLEO'S TARTAR SAUCE
1 1/2 cups mayonnaise
2 tablespoons sweet pickle relish OR 1- four ounce jar capers with juice
1/4 cup minced red onion
1 teaspoon lime juice
2 tablespoons chopped fresh parsley

### DIRECTIONS:
Make the tartar sauce ahead of time so it is well chilled. Combine all ingredients in sealable container and mix well. Refrigerate.

Heat 3 inches of oil in a deep skillet or deep fat fryer to 375 degrees. Fry chips until golden brown, then drain on brown paper bag and season with salt. Place potatoes on baking sheet lined with aluminum foil in a warm oven (200 degrees) while you cook the fish. Keep oil hot and add more if necessary to make 3 inches.

Wash fish with lime juice and water and pat dry. Season with salt and pepper. Combine all batter ingredients and mix until smooth. The batter should be thin. Dip each of the fillets into flour and then into the batter, then dip in the flour once again. Fry in hot oil for three to four minutes, or until crisp and golden brown. Do not overcrowd the pan when frying-it's important the oil is hot to cook fish properly so batter comes up crisp but fish is cooked inside. Drain on brown paper. Serve at once.

# Steam Fish

*This is a simple old time recipe and still the favorite Caymanian way to cook fish, but our steaming means something different. We used coconut oil, which is hard to find today and the flavor was so much better. The fish tasted just as good cold as hot! You sauté the vegetables first then lay the fish on top and cover and let it "steam."*

### INGREDIENTS:
2 pounds (4 -8 ounce) snapper, dolphin or other fish filets
Cold water and lime juice
2 tablespoons coconut oil or vegetable oil
Seasoned salt and black pepper
2 tablespoons chopped scallion
1 large onion, sliced thin
1 medium sweet green pepper, chopped
2 tablespoons water or chicken broth
1/2 teaspoon salt or Nature's Seasons
Few slices Cayman (Scotch bonnet) pepper, seeded

### DIRECTIONS:
You can leave the skin on if using small fish filets, otherwise, remove it. Wash the fish in cold water and lime juice and pat dry. Check over carefully and remove bones and cut away the dark flesh or bloodline. Season fish with seasoned salt and pepper. In a large heavy skillet, heat the coconut oil over medium high heat. Now this is where opinions differ. Some like to sauté the fish for a minute on each side so it absorbs the flavor of the oil, and then and add the onion and sweet pepper, water and remaining salt, and the Cayman pepper. Others cook the vegetables for a minute in the oil, then add the water and lay the fish on top. Either way, you then reduce heat to low and cover. Cook fish 10 minutes or until done.  Makes 4 servings.

*\*Today many Caymanians like to use Morton's Nature's Seasons seasoning blend instead of salt or seasoned salt. It is a nice mix of spices, including garlic, onion and celery and is not strong. You can find it in any supermarket spice section.*

# Steam Fish in Foil

If cooking fish filets or steaks in foil over a grill or fire: generously spray a piece of heavy foil with Pam or vegetable oil spray, or spread 2 teaspoons oil over foil to prevent sticking. Place sliced onion, sweet green pepper and 1 medium sliced tomato (if desired) on foil and lay fish on top. If not using tomato, which keeps the fish moist, then use 2 tablespoons of water or broth. Seal edges with a double fold. Place foil packages on hot grill and cook about 8 minutes, depending on size of packets. You can also cook the fish in the oven this way, at 400 F for about the same time.


# Cleo's Broiled Fish

You can use red snapper, dolphin fish or grouper for this recipe and it will be just as delicious.

Take a cleaned whole fish (make sure it is well cleaned and the skin left on but scales removed!) and split it in two large filets by removing the backbone. Place fish pieces, skin side down, on a greased broiling pan and brush with melted butter, then sprinkle with salt and black pepper. Lay strips of bacon over fish and broil for 8-10 minutes, then turn with skin side up and broil until skin is brown and crisp, about 10- 12 minutes, depending on size of fish. Save the drippings from the pan and spoon over the fish when serving. Garnish with lemon slices and a sprinkling of parsley. You can serve the fish with Mornay Sauce too, for a rich dish, but many like it this simple way, with pepper sauce if desired.

# Broiled Wahoo with Mornay Sauce

**INGREDIENTS:**
6 wahoo steaks or skinless filets, about 3/4 inch thick
Lime juice
Salt and black pepper
6 tablespoons melted butter or vegetable oil


**DIRECTIONS:**
Wash the wahoo pieces with cold water and lime juice and pat dry. Place on foil-lined broiler pan and brush tops generously with melted butter or oil to prevent drying out, then sprinkle with salt and pepper. Broil 6-8 minutes, until fish separates easily when prodded with a knife-no longer or fish will be too dry! Serve with Mornay Sauce.

# Mornay Sauce

*INGREDIENTS:*
4 tablespoons butter
4 tablespoons flour
2 cups cream (evaporated milk)
2 tablespoons shredded sharp cheddar cheese
1 tablespoon sherry

*DIRECTIONS:*
In small pan, melt the butter over medium low heat, then whisk in the flour until smooth. Cook one minute, but do not allow to brown, then whisk in cream until smooth. Stir in cheese and continue stirring until cheese melts and mixture is smooth, then stir in sherry. Cook until thickened, then remove from heat and spoon over fish.

# Barbecue Fish

Cooking fish any way takes a light hand, especially over an open fire. Even though I didn't cook on grill or barbecue myself, because I am so allergic to smoke, I prepared the fish or meat for the grill or fire.

You can make this simple sauce to use when grilling or broiling fish. It gives a good flavor without making a burnt crust from too much sugar, as most bottled barbecue sauces do. In Cayman, men do most of the barbequing and most cook white flesh fish tightly wrapped in foil on the fire. If you try to cook skinned fish open on the grill, it can easily fall apart. We would grill only steak fish, like queen fish (wahoo); kingfish (mackerel) or tuna, over the open flame.

# Simple Fish Basting Sauce

*Prepare the fish filets first by washing in cold water and lime juice and removing the skin and bloodline. If using on fish steaks, remove the bloodline only (the small triangle of fatty dark meat at the top where meat attaches to the bone.)*

### INGREDIENTS:
1 cup (2 sticks) butter or margarine, melted
1 teaspoon ground black pepper
1/2 teaspoon seasoned salt
½ teaspoon garlic salt
2 tablespoons Worcestershire sauce
6 tablespoons fresh lime juice
6 drops Angostura bitters

### DIRECTIONS:
Combine all ingredients and mix well. Brush fish filets or steaks, or other seafood (lobster or shrimp) generously before and during broiling or grilling.

# Fish "Cayman-Style"

*This is what people call Cayman style fish today, a recipe from Caymanian captains who made lunch for tourists on the beach. Back in the early 1950s, North Sound beach picnic trips were one of Cayman's first tourist activities. Conch and lobster, along with grouper, snapper or reef fish were caught. The raw conch was made into salad with lime and seasonings. The fish was cleaned and seasoned with lime, ketchup, onions, sweet peppers, Worcestershire, margarine and salt and pepper-sealed in foil and "steamed" over a fire or grill for about 20 minutes, until done. Caymanians cooking for themselves might add country pepper.*

**You can use any fish, but dolphin fish (mahi-mahi) and wahoo are very good.**

### INGREDIENTS:
4- 6 ounce fish steaks or fillets, bloodline and skin removed
3 fresh limes
Cold water
1 -2 teaspoons seasoned or garlic salt
2 teaspoons ground black pepper
1 large yellow onion, sliced thin (about 1-1/2 cups)
1 large green pepper, seeded and cored, sliced thin
3/4 cup ketchup
2 tablespoons Worcestershire sauce
½ -1 teaspoon dried thyme
Minced, seeded Scotch Bonnet pepper if desired, or hot sauce
4 tablespoons margarine, cut into piece

### DIRECTIONS:
Preheat oven to 350. Wash the fish with fresh lime juice and water. Season with seasoned or garlic salt and black pepper. Grease with margarine a large piece of foil and place the sliced onion, green pepper on top. Place the fish pieces on top of vegetables. Mix together the ketchup, Worcestershire sauce, thyme and pepper or hot sauce if desired, adjusting quantity of each to suit your taste. Spread sauce over fish, and top each piece with margarine. Make a packet of the foil and seal edges. Bake in oven or cook over grill fire for 20 -25 minutes or until fish separates easily when prodded with a fork.

# Fish Meuniere

*This is a French recipe with a delicious and simple lemon-butter sauce. It is like what we might call pan fried fish, using fresh local lime juice instead. Sometimes I would have imported sole to use at the Club, but this recipe is good with snapper, grouper and dolphin. Today you could use also tilapia. Use a light hand and be careful not to overcook.*

### INGREDIENTS:
1 cup flour
6 fish filets, about 6 ounces each, skin removed
Salt
Ground black pepper
3 tablespoons butter
3 tablespoons vegetable oil

Lemon or Lime butter sauce:
6 tablespoons butter
3 tablespoons fresh lemon or lime juice
Salt to taste
2 tablespoons fresh parsley, chopped

### DIRECTIONS:
Wash the fish in cold water and lime juice and pat dry, then season both sides of each piece with salt and pepper. Lay flat on plate and set aside. Spread the flour evenly in a shallow dish or plate. One at a time, coat each piece with a thin layer of flour, shaking off the excess, and lay on wax paper while pan is heating.

In a large (12 inch) skillet, heat 1 tablespoon oil until hot, then add 1 tablespoon butter, swirling pan so it melts evenly. Gently place two fish filets in pan and reduce heat to medium high. Cook 3 minutes and then carefully turn over and cook 3 minutes longer. Remove fish to platter and cover with foil. Wipe out pan and repeat all steps until all fish is cooked this way.

**For the sauce:** In another clean small skillet, melt the butter over medium heat and cook, swirling pan frequently, just until butter begins to brown lightly and smell nutty. Remove from heat and whisk in the lime juice until blended, and add salt to taste if desired. Spoon sauce over warm fish and sprinkle with parsley. Garnish with thin lemon or lime slices if you want. Serve at once.

# Baked Fish Au Gratin

*White cheddar cheese is best but you can use a good quality yellow cheddar too. Do not use processed American or Velveeta with this recipe!*

**INGREDIENTS:**

1/2 cup dry breadcrumbs
2 teaspoons melted butter
2 tablespoon grated white cheese
   (cheddar)
2 pounds fish filets
   (white fish, like dolphin or grouper)
½ teaspoon salt
½ teaspoon black pepper
½ teaspoon thyme

1 teaspoon paprika
1 cup grated white cheddar
   cheese, divided

1 cup chopped yellow onion
2 tablespoons butter
2 tablespoons flour
1/4 teaspoon salt
1/4 teaspoon black pepper
1 cup cream (evaporated milk)
2 tablespoons white wine

**DIRECTIONS:**

Preheat oven to 350 F. Butter or spray with Pam vegetable oil spray a deep 9 inch square baking dish. Make the topping: combine the first three ingredients, toss lightly and set aside. Wash the fish filets in cold water and lime and pat dry. Look over carefully to remove any bones! Cut the fish into 2- inch pieces and sprinkle all over with salt and pepper, thyme and paprika. (If you prefer, you can cut fish into larger pieces.)

In a large saucepan, melt the butter over medium heat and sauté the onions until soft. Sprinkle with flour, salt and pepper, and stir to blend. Cook 1 minute. Gradually add the cream, stirring constantly, until smooth and bring to a low boil. Cook 1 minute longer, until mixture thickens, then stir in wine and blend until smooth. Arrange half the seasoned fish in the baking dish, sprinkle with half the cheese and top with remaining fish and cheese. Pour the sauce over the fish and top with the breadcrumb cheese mixture. Back 35-40 minutes, until top is golden and casserole is bubbling. Remove from oven and let rest 10 minutes before serving. Makes 4 -6 servings.

# Fish Amandine

Follow recipe above, adding ½ cup sliced or slivered almonds and 1 minced garlic clove to the sauce recipe. Melt butter over medium heat and stir in almonds and garlic. Cook just until garlic is cooked and almonds begin to brown lightly-do not let butter scorch! Spoon over warm fish, sprinkle with parsley and serve immediately.

# Baked Stuffed Fish

*I was always very particular about serving fish with all the bones removed. When I made this dish, instead of stuffing a whole fish, I insisted on removing the head, backbone and skin and using only the large flat sides or filets. Everything could be eaten, the fish looked and tasted better and guests would not be offended by the sight of a fish head on their table. This recipe should serve 6, depending on the size of the cleaned fish. For a larger fish, double the stuffing recipe as needed.*

### INGREDIENTS:
1 6-8 pound red snapper or other white flesh fish
Salt and pepper (you can used seasoned or garlic salt if you prefer)
6 tablespoons margarine
4 slices bacon
Paprika

### STUFFING:
2 cups dry bread crumbs
¼ cup milk
2 tablespoons butter
1 small yellow onion, minced
1 stalk celery, chopped fine
½ teaspoon salt
¼ teaspoon black pepper
½ teaspoon ground sage
1 large egg, beaten
3 tablespoons margarine, cut into small pieces
6 slices bacon, cut in half
Paprika

## DIRECTIONS:

Preheat oven to 350F. Line a baking pan large enough to hold fish with foil and lightly oil or grease with margarine. Prepare the fish: remove the head, backbone, bloodline and skin, leaving two large filets. Wash well in cold water and lime juice and pat dry. Season fish with salt and pepper.

Place the breadcrumbs in a medium bowl and pour the milk over, then stir lightly. Let stand while preparing the other ingredients. In a small skillet, melt the butter over medium high heat and add the onion, cooking until it just begins to turn golden brown. Add the onion mixture to bread crumbs, and stir in celery and remaining ingredients and mix well. Spoon the stuffing evenly along the center of the bottom filet, leaving a half inch edge, and top with second filet. Press lightly to seal stuffing inside and dot top filet with margarine and lay bacon pieces across, evenly spaced. Sprinkle with paprika.

Bake fish uncovered for 45 minutes or until meat separates easily when prodded with a fork.

# Seafood Treasures

Imagine a time and place when lobster fresh from the sea was so plentiful it was poor man's food? That was Cayman years ago. Shrimp was a foreign delicacy from Honduras, but Cleo's generation remember lobster as common, even "poor man's" food, eaten steamed with lime juice and rice, or stewed in coconut milk and a little country pepper.

When the Tortuga Club opened, foreign guests discovered a gourmand's paradise. Most seafood was fresh from local waters, with the exception of scallops and shrimp, which had to be imported. Lobster was a delicacy enjoyed back home only on special occasions at elegant restaurants. But the sweet taste and delicate texture of fresh Caribbean spiny lobster came as a surprise to visitors, who had only tasted its tougher and less tasty North American cousin, Maine lobster.

You should know our laws regulating Cayman's Lobster Season. The local population of this prized crustacean is rapidly decreasing and most of what is served locally is imported from other Caribbean countries. In fact, spiny lobster is now a delicacy in Cayman. Under the current marine conservation laws in the Cayman Islands, lobster season is only open from Dec. 1 until February 28, and the limit is three per person or six per boat per day, with a minimum tail length of 6 inches. In addition, you cannot purchase or receive as a gift more than three lobsters per day from Cayman waters during open season.

# Lobster Thermidor

*This is still considered a fancy dish today and is very rich. It is not hard to make. Don't use cheap cooking sherry, use real brandy or sherry, and pre-cook the lobster until almost done, but not hard and rubbery. Today, some chefs would insist that you don't use only heavy cream, and not broth, onion or flour, and reduce the sauce until thickened. But this is how I made mine and it was a hit with guests. Some even said that I knew how to cook better than the French! This recipe serves 4-6.*

**INGREDIENTS:**

4 lobster tails (8 ounces each)
Key lime juice
½ cup butter
1 cup white mushrooms,
  sliced thin
¼ cup white or yellow
  onion, diced
¼ cup flour
1/4 cup brandy or cognac

½ cup sherry
1/4 cup chicken broth
1-3/4 cups evaporated milk
  or light cream
3 large egg yolks, beaten
1 teaspoon salt
½ teaspoon black pepper
1 teaspoon paprika
4 tablespoons buttered breadcrumbs
4 tablespoons parmesan cheese

**DIRECTIONS:**

Split the lobster tails lengthwise and wash with cold water and lime juice to remove any grit or guts. Place in a large saucepan with just enough water to steam, and add juice of one key lime to water. Cover and steam 2-3 minutes, until lobster is barely cooked--turning translucent but not hard and white. Remove from heat and cool in shells. When lobster is cool enough to handle, remove from shells and cut into ½ inch pieces. Save shells if you want to serve the thermidor in shells instead of scallop baking dishes.

In a large saucepan (3 quart), melt butter over medium heat and sauté the onion and mushrooms until turning soft but not brown. Sprinkle flour over vegetables and stir, then reduce heat to low and cook one minute. Remove from heat and stir in brandy and broth, then return to heat, bring to a boil. Stir in cream and immediately reduce heat to low.

Place beaten egg yolks in a small bowl and whisk in enough of the hot cream mixture to warm the yolks. Pour the yolk mixture into the cream mixture in the saucepan and heat, stirring or whisking frequently over low heat, until sauce thickens—do not allow to boil. Add salt, pepper and paprika, then gently stir in the lobster meat, stirring until pieces are coated. Add additional salt and pepper if desired.

Heat oven to 350F.  Divide lobster thermidor among the shell halves or in four lightly greased scallop baking dishes or ramekins and place on baking sheet. Sprinkle each top with breadcrumbs and cheese, if desired—this might be too rich for your taste. Bake for 15 minutes, or until tops are just turning golden brown.

According to culinary lore, Lobster Thermidor was created at a Parisian restaurant, Chez Maize on January 24, 1894 for opening night of Thermidor, a play by Parisian Victorian Sardou. The highly controversial theatrical production opened and closed the same night—unlike its culinary namesake, which has been a hit for over a century.

# Lobster (Shrimp) Newburg

*I read that this dish that put New York's Delmonico's restaurant on the map-back in 1895! Newburg is a rich but simple sauce, made with sherry, butter, cream, egg yolks and a pinch of red pepper-never with brandy or cognac. It has many variations today, including the addition of shallots, onion, pimiento and even mushrooms. But this is the original recipe, subtle and simple-it should not be like an A La King casserole.*

**INGREDIENTS:**

3 lobster tails
  (8 ounces each) or 1-1/2 pounds
  raw large shrimp (for 3 cups)
Key lime juice
6 tablespoons butter
2 tablespoons flour
1 teaspoon salt

½ teaspoon black pepper
¼ teaspoon cayenne pepper or
  hot pepper sauce
3 tablespoons sherry
2 cups light cream
3 large egg yolks, beaten
½ teaspoon paprika

**DIRECTIONS:**

If using lobster, split the lobster tails lengthwise and wash with cold water and lime juice to remove any grit or guts. For shrimp, wash as above and remove heads and legs if still on. Place in a large saucepan with just enough water to steam, and add juice of one key lime to water. Cover and steam 2-3 minutes, until lobster is barely cooked--turning milky but not hard. Remove from heat and cool in shells. When cool enough to handle, remove shellfish from shells and cut into ½ inch pieces. Some chefs prefer to slice the lobster meat, medallion style, into ¼ inch rounds.

In a medium saucepan, melt the butter over low heat and sprinkle in the flour, stirring well, then add salt and peppers. Stir in sherry and cream and stir well and heat through. Place egg yolks in small bowl and gradually stir in enough cream mixture to warm the egg yolks, then return this to saucepan and blend well. Stir in the shellfish and cook over low heat, stirring slowly, until sauce just thickens, then spoon over toast points or fluffy white rice, or into puff pastry shells and sprinkle with paprika.

# Lobster Washington

*This is a rich recipe that is very filling and especially good if served over brown rice.*

**INGREDIENTS:**
6 - 8-inch lobster tails
¾ cup (1-1/2 sticks) butter
¾ cup flour
6 cups cream (evaporated milk)
3 tablespoons butter
1 cup sliced white mushrooms
½ cup chopped onion
1 small (4 ounce) jar diced pimentos
¼ cup cooking sherry

**DIRECTIONS:**
Boil or steam the lobster tails in the shell until they turn opaque and are just done, about 10 minutes—do not overcook until dry and tough! Let cool, then remove meat from shells and slice crosswise into medallions or cut into small pieces. Set aside.

In large saucepan, melted ¾ cup butter over medium heat, then sprinkle with flour and stir until smooth. Reduce heat to medium low and cook until mixture turns ivory, stirring frequently. Gradually stir in the milk (a wire whisk works best) until smooth. Cook, stirring constantly, until mixture thickens. Remove from heat.

In medium skillet, melt raining 3 tablespoons butter and add mushrooms, onion and pimento. Stir and sauté until vegetables are soft and mushroom has released most of their liquid. Stir sautéed vegetables into cream sauce, then add lobster pieces and sherry. Stir well and heat over low heat until mixture is hot but not boiling. Serve over brown rice and sprinkle with grated cheddar cheese if desired. Makes 8- 10 servings.

# Lobster Delight

*This recipe makes good use of the lobster meat that can be picked from the head, body shells and legs, sometimes called "head meat" which is too often thrown away today. It is nice for parties where guests serve themselves. Artichoke hearts are a modern "gourmet" touch and can be left out to suit your taste.*

### INGREDIENTS:
4 cups lobster meat, cooked and diced
2-1/2 cups cooked white rice
2 tablespoons lime juice
½ cup butter
3 tablespoons minced onion
½ cup flour
4 cups light cream
½ cup white wine or dry sherry
1 teaspoon ground black pepper
1 teaspoon garlic salt
1 8-ounce jar diced pimentos, drained
2- 14- ounce cans quartered artichoke hearts (optional) well drained
2-1/2 cups grated Swiss cheese, parmesan or mixture of both
Paprika

### DIRECTIONS:
*Preheat oven to 350 F. Lightly butter or spray with Pam a large (4 quart) baking dish and spread the rice evenly over bottom. Pick over the lobster meat carefully, to be sure all shell pieces are removed and sprinkle with lime juice. Set aside. Sauté the onions in butter until just turning soft. Sprinkle flour over onions and stir to blend; cook until mixture is pale golden in color, then remove from heat.*

*In a medium saucepan, heat cream just until it begins to boil and add slowly to flour mixture, stirring until well blended. Return to heat and cook, stirring, until mixture begins to simmer. Reduce heat and stir in wine or sherry, salt and pepper, until smooth and cook until mixture thickens, stirring constantly. Drain off any lime juice from the lobster meat and gently stir into cream sauce, then add pimentos, artichokes, and ½ cup of the cheese. Pour into prepared baking dish. Sprinkle remaining cheese evenly over top, (use more if you like a thicker topping) then dust with paprika. Bake at 350° for 25 to 30 minutes, until cheese is lightly browned and casserole is bubbling. Serves 8.*

# Cleo's Crab Newburg

*This is similar to the simple, original recipe, which many have complicated over the last century to include green and red peppers, onions, mushrooms, cheese and so forth.*

*I used tinned imported crab meat, not local land crab or sea crabs. And that fake crabmeat (Surimi) sold today is not a good substitute for anything and never had found a place in my kitchen!*

**INGREDIENTS:**
**2 tablespoons butter**
**2 tablespoons flour**
**1/4 teaspoon salt**
**2 cups cream (evaporated milk) or light cream**
**2 tablespoons sherry**
**1 teaspoon dry mustard**
**2 large egg yolks, beaten**
**1 pound cooked crabmeat (you can substitute peeled cooked shrimp)**
**½ cup fine breadcrumbs**
**2 tablespoons butter, cut into small pieces**
**Paprika**

**DIRECTIONS:**
Preheat oven to 350. Lightly butter a 1-1/2 quart baking dish. In a double boiler over simmering water, melt butter and stir in flour. Cook, stirring constantly to prevent lumps, about two minutes-do not allow to brown-then add salt and stir well. Add cream and sherry and whisk until smooth. Reduce heat to low. Stir a few tablespoons of the cream mixture into the egg yolks and blend well, then add to cream sauce and stir well. Stir in mustard and sherry. Cook 3-4 minutes, or until thickened, but do not allow to boil and remove from heat. Stir in crabmeat. Pour crab mixture into buttered casserole or four individual shell baking dishes. Sprinkle with breadcrumbs and dot with butter. Bake at 350 for 30 minutes until browned and bubbling. Dust tops with paprika for color if desired. Makes 4 -6 servings.

# Shrimp

Shrimp is not local seafood in Cayman and must be imported. At Tortuga Club, we would import big bags of frozen shrimp and that was a delicacy in those days. Today fresh shrimp comes in from Honduras from time to time, but the supermarket is still the only reliable source of previously frozen "fresh" shrimp. Shrimp is one of the easiest things to cook but many cooks make the mistake of overcooking it until it is rubbery and tasteless.

# Boiled Shrimp

*This sounds like an easy dish, and it is. The hard thing is to make people understand how to cook shrimp properly because most cook them way too long. It only takes a few minutes. Wash the shrimp in cold water and lime juice but do not remove the shells. Cooking shrimp in the shells gives them much better flavor. Many people like to peel their own shrimp but if not, peel them before serving. This makes 3-4 servings depending on how much your guests like shrimp.*

### INGREDIENTS:
2 quarts water
2 large limes, quartered
1 small onion, chopped
1-1/2 tablespoons salt
1 3-ounce package shrimp and crab boil
2 pounds unpeeled large shrimp, heads removed

### DIRECTIONS:
Combine all ingredients except shrimp in a large saucepan or Dutch oven and bring to a boil. Reduce heat to medium high and cover; simmer for 5 minutes to let the seasonings cook into the water. Uncover and stir in shrimp; bring to a boil, then immediately remove pan from heat and cover again. Let stand for 10-12 minutes until shrimp turn pink-stir, cover and let stand a few minutes longer if necessary. Drain shrimp, discarding seasonings and serve chilled with red sauce or peel and use in Shrimp Salad.

# Fried Shrimp in Beer Batter

*This easy recipe cooks up light and crisp but the shrimp stay full of flavor and tender.*

**INGREDIENTS:**
1 pound large fresh shrimp, unpeeled
Lime juice
1/4 cup flour
1 cup cornstarch
½ teaspoon baking powder
1/8 teaspoon salt
1/4 cup beer
2 tablespoons butter, melted
1 egg yolk, beaten
Vegetable oil

**DIRECTIONS:**
Rinse the shrimp in cold water with a little lime and pat dry. Peel shrimp, leaving tails on. In small bowl, combine flour, cornstarch, baking powder and salt and mix well. Stir in beer, butter and egg yolk and mix until smooth.

Pour oil to depth of 2 inches into a large heavy saucepan or skillet; heat to 375 F. or very hot-until a drop of batter sizzles rapidly. Use tongs to dip each shrimp into batter, and let excess drip back into bowl. Drop shrimp in hot oil and fry 2-3 minutes or until golden, turning gently if necessary for even cooking. Be careful not to crowd the shrimp in the pot or oil will not stay hot enough to fry properly. Drain shrimp on paper towels or brown paper bag and serve hot with tartar sauce or cocktail sauce. Makes 2-3 generous main course servings or 4 appetizer servings.

# Shrimp and Crab Au Gratin

## INGREDIENTS:

1 pound crab meat
2 pounds peeled uncooked shrimp
1/4 cup butter
1 rib celery, diced
2 medium yellow onions, chopped
2 scallions, chopped
1 clove garlic, minced
1 14 ounce can cream of mushroom soup
½ cup cream (evaporated milk) or half and half
1 teaspoon black pepper
1 8 ounce can mushroom stems and pieces, well-drained
½ cup white wine
2 tablespoons parsley
1 cup grated cheddar or parmesan cheese
1 cup buttered bread crumbs

## DIRECTIONS:

Pick over the crabmeat and shrimp to check for and remove any pieces of shell. In a large saucepan, melt butter over medium heat and add onions, scallion, celery and garlic and cook until vegetables are almost soft. Add shrimp, stirring to blend, and cook just until shrimp begin to turn pink, about two minutes longer. Stir in crabmeat, soup, cream, pepper and blend well. Cook, stirring several times, for another minute, then stir in mushrooms, parsley and wine, and then the cheese.

Preheat oven to 400 F. Pour mixture into a lightly buttered 2 quart baking dish. Sprinkle top evenly with breadcrumbs and bake 12-15 minutes or until top is lightly browned and mixture is bubbling. Serve with hot fluffy white rice.

# Shrimp Newburg

*Condensed soups that could be used instead of making white sauce from scratch made life a lot easier in the 1960's, when casseroles and entrees with cream sauces were popular. This recipe is quick and easy-and even faster if you leave off the topping and spoon the Newburg over toast points or white rice.*

### INGREDIENTS:

1 pound peeled, cooked shrimp
2 tablespoons butter
¼ cup yellow onion, chopped
¼ cup green sweet pepper, chopped
2 cans cream of shrimp soup
1 cup cream (evaporated milk) or half and half
1 small (4 ounce) jar chopped pimiento
1 8 ounce can sliced mushrooms, drained well
3 large egg yolks beaten
¼ cup sherry
½ teaspoon black pepper
1 cup buttered breadcrumbs
6 tablespoons finely grated parmesan or cheddar cheese

### DIRECTIONS:

Pick over shrimp carefully and remove any pieces of shell. In a large saucepan, melt the butter over medium heat and add the onion and sweet pepper. Cook until vegetables are just turning soft, then stir in the soup and cream and blend well. Stir in pimiento, shrimp and mushrooms and cook over medium low heat until mixture begins to bubble, then reduce heat to low. Stir 2 tablespoons of sauce into beaten eggs and blend well, then add mixture to sauce and cook three minutes longer. Stir in the sherry and pepper and continue cooking for five minutes, stirring several times.

Heat oven to 350 F. Divide Newburg among 6 baking dishes or ramekins and top with sprinkling of breadcrumbs and cheese. Bake for 15 minutes, or until mixture is bubbling and tops are lightly browned. Serve with white rice.

# Shrimp Creole

*Use tomato sauce, not tomato paste, for your Creole. And don't overcook the shrimp! And this recipe is also delicious if made with conch-tenderized first, cut into small pieces and cooked, then added to the Creole sauce and heated through. Some people insist the shrimp must be deveined, but I didn't bother. This makes 6 servings.*

### INGREDIENTS:
2-1/2 pounds raw peeled large shrimp
¼ cup butter or bacon fat
1/3 cup flour
1 medium onion, peeled and chopped
1 small green sweet pepper, seeded and chopped
1 stalk celery, diced
2 cloves garlic, minced
1 teaspoon seasoned salt or Season All
1 teaspoon ground black pepper
1 (14 ounce) can tomato sauce
1 (14 ounce) can stewed tomatoes, undrained
½ teaspoon thyme
1 bay leaf
2 teaspoons sugar
Hot pepper sauce to taste (Tabasco or our own—better!)
2 tablespoons fresh chopped parsley

### DIRECTIONS:
In a large skillet, heat the butter or fat over medium heat and sauté the shrimp for two minutes, until just turning pink. Remove shrimp from pan and cover. Add the flour to pan and cook, stirring frequently, until turning golden brown, then stir in onions, sweet pepper, celery, garlic, salt and pepper. Cook 3 minutes, stirring frequently, until vegetables are turning soft, then add tomato sauce and tomatoes, thyme and bay leaf. Stir well, then cover, reduce heat to low and simmer for 30 minutes to develop flavors. Add shrimp and cook until shrimp are heated through and pink, another minute or two. Add pepper sauce to taste, if desired and sprinkle with parsley. Serve over hot fluffy white rice.

*\*\* You can also cook the shrimp in the sauce at the end instead of sautéing first. Add the shrimp to the simmering sauce and cook for 3 minutes, until they are pink but not rubbery!*

# Shrimp Salad

*This is an easy dish to make-but be careful with the dressing. The amount of mayonnaise to use is a matter of taste, but too much makes a sloppy dish and smothers the taste of the shrimp. You can also add a tablespoon or more of chopped sweet pickles or sliced olives if you want. This makes four servings.*

### INGREDIENTS:
3 cups cooked shrimp
1 tablespoon fresh lime juice
1 cup celery, diced
2 scallions, chopped
1 tablespoon chili sauce or ketchup
1/2 cup mayonnaise
½ teaspoon Worcestershire sauce
½ teaspoon seasoned salt
½ teaspoon black pepper
Tabasco or Cayman pepper sauce to taste
Paprika

### DIRECTIONS:
If the shrimp are large, cut into smaller pieces. Combine the first four ingredients in a medium bowl and toss lightly. Blend chili sauce, mayonnaise and remaining seasonings, then stir gently into shrimp mixture. Add more mayonnaise if desired. Chill thoroughly and spoon onto lettuce leaves; sprinkle with paprika for color before serving.

# Meat Dishes from Around the World

When I started working at Tortuga Club in 1964, beef and pork were still very special foods and most Caymanians, including my family, usually ate them only at Christmas time. I didn't know about all those different kinds or cuts of meat, and had no idea about the many meat recipes from around the world. It was exciting for me to learn to cook so many new dishes. It wasn't long before local people heard about the "gourmet restaurant" at Tortuga Club in East End. Each week we had many dinner guests who drove from all over Cayman.

# Old Fashioned Beef Stew

*The flavor of this favorite dish is even better if reheated the next day.*

## INGREDIENTS:
2 pounds boneless beef chuck roast, cut into 2 inch pieces
1 teaspoon salt
1 teaspoon pepper
2 teaspoons paprika
½ cup flour
¼ cup vegetable or olive oil
2 medium yellow onions, diced
1 medium sweet green pepper, chopped
2 stalks celery, sliced
4 cups beef broth
2 teaspoons browning or Kitchen bouquet
2 tablespoons Worcestershire sauce
1 bay leaf
2 teaspoons garlic salt
1 teaspoon seasoned salt
1 teaspoon black pepper
2 large carrots, peeled and sliced (divided)
2 medium Irish potatoes, peeled and diced (about 2 cups)
1 -2 cups additional beef broth

## DIRECTIONS:
Season the meat on all sides with the salt, pepper and paprika. Sprinkle pieces evenly with flour. Heat oil in Dutch oven and add meat; brown the meat all over, cooking in batches, until well browned. Add onions, sweet pepper and celery and stir mixture well. Cook over medium heat for 2 minutes, stirring several times, then add beef broth, browning, Worcestershire sauce and bay leaf. Stir well, cover and bring to a boil, then reduce heat to a low simmer and cover. Cook 2 hours, stirring occasionally, until meat is almost fork tender. Add potatoes and carrots, and additional beef broth if stew is becoming too dry, and stir well and cook uncovered 20 minutes longer, until vegetables are soft. Thicken stew gravy to desired thickness by mixing 2 tablespoons flour with ¼ cup cold water. Stir into stew until blended and cook 5 minutes longer until gravy is thickened.

# Pot Roast with Tomato Gravy

*This is another "slow cooking" recipe, American comfort food from decades ago, when braising (cooking cheaper cuts of meats slowly in a small amount of liquid to make them tender) was the way many people cooked. Braising creates many delicious dishes but it takes time.*

**INGREDIENTS:**

1 - 3-1/2 to 4 pound boneless chuck roast
1/2 cup flour
1 teaspoon seasoned or regular salt
½ teaspoon pepper
¼ teaspoon paprika
2 tablespoons vegetable oil
1 large onion, quartered and sliced
1 cup beef broth
1 can (10-3/4 ounces) condensed tomato soup
2 fresh thyme sprigs
1 teaspoon black pepper
1 teaspoon garlic powder
1 teaspoon salt
3 large carrots, sliced thick
4 medium Irish potatoes, peeled and quartered

**DIRECTIONS:**

Place roast on a large plate. Combine flour, salt, pepper and paprika and sprinkle over roast, rubbing into surface and turning to coast all sides. In large Dutch oven (5-6 quart) heat oil over medium high heat until hot then reduce heat to medium and brown roast slowly on all sides. Add sliced onions and stir to distribute evenly; cook until onions are turning soft, then add all remaining ingredients except carrots and potatoes. When mixture comes to a boil, reduce heat to low, cover and cook just at a low simmer for 2-1/2 to 3 hours, or until meat is fork tender. Check occasionally and stir, to prevent anything from sticking to bottom and add a little broth if liquid has cooked away too much. When meat is very tender, remove roast from pan and place on serving platter, covered with foil. Remove thyme sprig and add vegetables to cooking liquid; cook 15-20 minutes or until tender.

**Gravy:** when vegetables are tender, remove with slotted spoon to serving platter and thicken gravy if necessary: combine 1 tablespoon cornstarch mixed with 2 tablespoons water until smooth. Stir into roast liquid and cook over medium high heat until mixture thickens, about 3-4 minutes. Add more salt and pepper to taste, if necessary.

"Irish potatoes" are what Caymanians call plain white potatoes, to distinguish them from our local sweet potatoes, yams and other starchy tubers. Local people consider them dull, almost a last resort if a starch is needed in a recipe. We would rather have ground provisions like breadfruit, coco and yam.

# Beef Beaujolais
# (Bourguignon)

*When I first learned how to make this French dish, it was considered a gourmet recipe and guests would ask me how I knew about things! You can serve it over white rice or plain boiled egg noodles.*

### INGREDIENTS:
2 tablespoons oil
8 ounces bacon, coarsely chopped
2 pounds boneless beef chuck, cut into 1 1/2-inch cubes
Salt and black pepper for seasoning beef
1/2 cup flour
1 large onion, chopped
2 large garlic cloves, peeled and crushed (left whole)
3 fresh thyme sprigs or 1-1/2 teaspoons dried thyme
1/3 cup fresh parsley
½ teaspoon salt
½ teaspoon black pepper
1 cup canned beef broth
1-2 cups cup red Burgundy wine
1/2 pound small mushrooms, whole

### DIRECTIONS:
Place oil and bacon in heavy large Dutch oven and cook over medium heat until brown and crisp, about 8 minutes. Using slotted spoon, remove bacon to paper towels. Season beef pieces generously with salt and pepper; coat with flour, using all of flour. Working in batches, brown beef in same pot over medium-high heat, turning pieces as they are well-browned, about 10 minutes per batch. Add a little more oil if needed to cook meat properly. Transfer browned meat to large bowl. Reduce heat to medium and add onion, garlic, thyme, bay leaf, parsley, and remaining salt and pepper to same pot and cook, stirring several times, until onion softens. Be careful not to scorch the garlic.

Add 1 cup broth and 1 cup wine to pot, scraping up browned bits, about 8 minutes. Return meat and its juices to pot. Stir gently. Bring to boil, stirring occasionally. Reduce heat to low, until just simmering gently, cover pot and cook for an hour. Uncover and add mushrooms and bacon pieces. Stir gently and add a little more wine (or beef broth) if the mixture looks too dry. Cover and cook until beef is tender and liquid is reduced and thickened—this will depend on the meat, but it could be as little as 30 minutes. Adjust salt and pepper if necessary. Serves 4 but you can easily double this recipe for a larger crowd.

# Cleo's Irish Roots

My people go all the way back to Ireland. On my father's side, my great grandfather was an Irishman named John Jarrett Conolly. We never could find out what brought him to Grand Cayman-and especially, all the way to East End! He was a real pioneer. My father's mother was an O'Connor. My great grandmother from my mother's side was a Hunter from the Brac.

So on St. Patrick's Day at the Club, I would have corned beef and cabbage on the menu and tell people I was Irish too and this always surprised them and made their eyes grow big. They didn't know what to say. Now, my family didn't celebrate St. Patrick's Day and this dish wasn't something we ate at home when I was growing up! A little piece of salt beef in coconut milk, or rundown, is the closest thing we had to that, because any kind of meat was dear.

# Corned Beef and Cabbage

*I used to make this on St. Patrick's Day as a surprise for guests and there were never any leftovers. Except for one year, and I forget what that was. I had my dates wrong and served corned beef and cabbage a day late. Those guests wouldn't eat it! Not a bite! I have never been able to figure out why. But there were always funny things like that happening. Today you will find that many people in Cayman enjoy this dish-not only on St. Patrick's Day. Year-round you will see it on local take away menus.*

*Be sure your cabbage is bright green and fresh. If old, it will be pale, taste bitter and ruin your dinner. Don't rush this dish. Cook the meat until it is fork tender, which will take several hours depending on the size of the piece of meat. Then be sure to carve the meat cross the grain.*

INGREDIENTS:
1 -5 pound corned beef brisket, trimmed of excess fat
3 cloves garlic, chopped
1 medium onion, quartered
8 small onions, quartered
10 medium carrots, peeled and quartered
4 large white Irish potatoes, peeled and quartered
1 medium head cabbage, cut into 8 pieces

DIRECTIONS:
Place meat in Dutch oven or large pot and cover with cold water. Add garlic and the quartered onion, and bring to a boil. Reduce heat to simmer, cover and cook about 3-1/2 – 4 hours, or until meat is fork tender. Remove meat to platter and cover with foil. Remove cooked onion, skim off any fat that has risen to the top of the liquid, then add vegetables and return to a boil. Reduce heat to medium and cook, uncovered until vegetables are tender or the way you like them, about 20 -25 minutes.

# Cleo's Meat Loaf

*My meat loaf was always popular at the Club because it was so moist and flavorful. I usually served it with mashed potatoes and buttered carrots. Many people here in Cayman still love meat loaf today but you seldom see it on menus. You can add more seasoning, like minced country pepper, if you wish. This is not a large recipe and can be doubled if you want leftovers.*

### INGREDIENTS:

1/2 teaspoon garlic powder
½ teaspoon celery salt
1/2 teaspoon black pepper
1 teaspoon salt
1 teaspoon dry mustard
2 tablespoons dried parsley
1/2 cup cream (evaporated milk)
2 cups homemade breadcrumbs
2 large eggs, lightly beaten
3/4 cup finely diced onion
1/4 cup finely diced sweet pepper
2 tablespoons A-1 or similar Steak Sauce
2 pounds ground beef (chuck is best)
1/4 cup ketchup
4 strips bacon, cut in half
Additional ground black pepper

### DIRECTIONS:

Preheat oven to 375 F. Spray a 9 x 9 inch baking pan with vegetable spray or line with foil. In a large mixing bowl, combine all ingredients except the beef, ketchup and bacon and stir to mix. Crumble in the beef and use your hands to mix, just until all ingredients are blended--do not over mix or the meatloaf will be too firm.

Shape mixture into a loaf (about 9 inches by 6 inches) pressing firmly, and place in prepared pan. Top with bacon slices and spread ketchup evenly over bacon. Sprinkle with additional black pepper. Bake at 375 for about an hour. Remove from oven, drain off fat and let meat rest for 10 -15 minutes before slicing. Meatloaf should be firm but still ooze some juices.

# Cleo's Coffee Roasted Leg of Lamb

Guests were surprised by lamb cooked this way, and loved the taste. As unusual as the combination of seasonings in this recipe sounds, they cook down into a delicious gravy. Coffee cuts the fat and the gamey taste in the lamb. Not many could guess the secret ingredient. Leg of lamb and other lamb roasts are covered with a thin membrane (called the "fell"). Don't remove this! It helps the lamb keep its shape and stay juicier.

**INGREDIENTS:**
1 5 pound leg of lamb (sirloin is best)
2 tablespoons vegetable oil
Salt and fresh ground black pepper
2 sprigs fresh mint, crumbled
6 cups brewed coffee, at room temperature
2 cups milk
¼ cup red wine
2 tablespoons mint jelly
2 tablespoons flour

**DIRECTIONS:**
Preheat oven to 350 F. Rub roast all over with oil and season well with salt and pepper and crumbled mint leaves. Place the meat fat side up on a rack in shallow roasting pan and roast uncovered for 30 minutes.

While roast is cooking, whisk together coffee, milk and red wine. After roast has cooked 30 minutes, remove from oven and pour coffee mixture evenly over roast. Return to oven and cook 2-1/2 to 3 hours, basting with sauce several times. Cooking time depends on desired degree of doneness. Figure on 20 minutes per pound for medium rare, 25 for well done. If using a meat thermometer, the reading should be 150 for rare, 160 -170 for medium and 175 to 180 F for well done.

Remove roast from oven and place on serving plate; cover loosely with foil and let stand 15-20 minutes before carving. Pour drippings and juices from pan into saucepan and stir well. Keep warm over low heat. To thicken sauce, stir enough water into 2 tablespoons flour to make a smooth paste, then stir into sauce in pan. Bring to a simmer and cook stirring several times, for five minutes longer, or until thickened. Add 2 tablespoons mint jelly and stir until smooth. Serve over lamb. You can also serve mint jelly on the side. This makes 6 servings.

Lamb roasted with coffee is actually a traditional, old Swedish recipe with many variations that have appeared in European cookbooks dating back to the early 1900s.

# Steak & Kidney Pie

*Maybe they didn't know what they were eating, but guests liked this dish so much, they always asked for more.*

## INGREDIENTS:

2 pounds beef round steak or stew beef, trimmed of excess fat
4 pounds beef or lamb kidneys
3 tablespoons reserved beef fat
2 medium yellow onions, quartered and sliced
1 tablespoon butter
2 cups boiling water
1-1/2/ tablespoons Worcestershire sauce
2 tablespoons parsley
1 teaspoon salt
1 teaspoon ground black pepper
2 tablespoons water
2 tablespoons flour

## AUTHENTIC SHORT CRUST PASTRY TOPPING:

(This must be chilled for at least 30 minutes. Make it while the meat is cooking)

2-1/2 cups flour
¼ teaspoon salt
6 tablespoons butter, cut into pieces
1/2 cup lard, cut into pieces
1 tablespoon confectioner's sugar
1 egg yolk, beaten
3 tablespoons cold water

## GLAZE:
2 tablespoons milk
1 beaten egg

## DIRECTIONS:

Slice the beef into 1" x 1/2 inch pieces or chunks and trim off excess fat, reserving 3 tablespoons. Wash the kidneys well in cold water and remove the outer membrane. Cut kidneys through the center lengthwise and remove fat and white tissue. Cut into ¼ inch pieces. Put the beef fat in a large heavy skillet or Dutch oven and heat over medium heat. Add the onions and cook, stirring several times, until just turning brown, then add the butter and cut meats and stir well. Brown meat well all over, but do not scorch. Add the boiling water, Worcestershire sauce, parsley, salt and pepper. Stir to mix and cover. Reduce heat to low and simmer 1-1/2 to 2 hours, stirring occasionally, until meat is fork tender. Add a little water from time to time if liquid cooks away too much-there must be enough to simmer meats and make rich gravy. (While meat is cooking, make the pastry crust. See below) When meat is tender, mix together water and flour and stir into meat and cook until remaining juices have thickened into a nice gravy. Remove from heat.

Preheat oven to 400 F. Divide the meat mixture among small greased individual baking dishes (I used ones that held enough for two people) or spoon all into one large baking dish. Cover meat evenly with crust and bake at 400 for 20-25 minutes until crust is golden brown. If this recipe is too much work, you can use your favorite pie crust recipe. Some prefer to top the pie with freshly made mashed potatoes or biscuit dough, which are also good, but the dish is best with a flaky pastry crust. Makes 8 servings.

**Make the Crust:**
Sift flour and salt into medium mixing bowl. Cut the butter and lard into the flour using a pastry blender or fork and then use your fingertips to rub into flour thoroughly, until mixture resembles coarse crumbs. Blend in the sugar. Mix egg yolk with water and blend into flour mixture until mixture forms a soft dough. Turn dough onto lightly floured surface and knead a few times until smooth. Wrap in plastic wrap or wax paper and chill for 30 minutes or longer. Roll the pastry out into size needed to cover individual dishes or large baking dish. Prick pasty with fork in center to allow steam to escape. Make the glaze: combine milk and egg and blend well, then brush pastry with mixture. Bake as above.

# *Ham Loaf*

*This is an old recipe that is still a favorite in Midwestern USA states like Kansas and Iowa especially. You can top with tomato sauce if you want, or a cheese sauce. It is just as delicious served by itself with corn pudding and buttered green beans.*

*INGREDIENTS:*
1 pound ground ham
   (smoked or other cooked variety)
1 pound ground pork
1 cup soft bread crumbs
2 large eggs, lightly beaten
½ cup cream (evaporated milk)
½ cup chopped green pepper
1 teaspoon dry mustard
   (Coleman's is good)

½ teaspoon salt
½ teaspoon ground black pepper
½ teaspoon paprika

*MUSTARD SAUCE:*
1 cup light brown sugar
2 tablespoons prepared
   (or 2 teaspoons dry) mustard
1/3 cup cider vinegar
1/3 cup water

*DIRECTIONS:*
Preheat oven to 350 F. In a large bowl, combine all ingredients for ham loaf (ham through pepper) and mix lightly, just until ingredients are combined-do not over mix. Line a shallow 9 inch square baking pan with foil and shape mixture into a loaf. Place in pan and sprinkle top with paprika and additional pepper if desired. Bake at 350F for 45 minutes.

While ham loaf is baking, make the sauce: combine all ingredients in small saucepan and stir well, bring to a boil, stirring several times, then reduce heat to medium and cook five minutes longer. Remove from heat and cool. At the end of 45 minutes, open oven and baste ham loaf generously all over with mustard sauce. Bake 45 minutes longer, basting once or twice with remaining sauce. Remove from oven and let stand for 10 minutes before serving. Makes 8 servings.

# Oven Baked Beef Roast

*This oven baked recipe is also called Yankee Pot Roast and cooked with just enough liquid to braise the roast. You make the gravy from the pan drippings after. If you refrigerate the leftover roast overnight, it slices easily for sandwiches.*

### INGREDIENTS:

1 -5 pound beef chuck roast (sirloin tip or rump roast are also good)
1/2 cup flour
1 teaspoon seasoned or regular salt
½ teaspoon pepper
¼ teaspoon paprika
2 tablespoons vegetable oil
1 cup beef broth
4 large Irish potatoes, peeled and quartered
8 medium carrots, peeled and sliced
6 small onions, peeled and sliced
1 cup sliced mushrooms
1 teaspoons salt
1 teaspoon black pepper

### DIRECTIONS:

Preheat oven to 350F. Combine flour, salt, pepper and paprika in small bowl and blend well. Sprinkle over entire surface of beef roast and rub in well. Heat oil in a Dutch oven until hot and brown roast on all sides. Add 1 cup beef broth and stir to loosen any browned pieces from bottom. Cover and bake 3 hours, turning roast twice and adding more broth if necessary. About 45 minutes before meat is done (it should be fork tender), arrange vegetables around meat and spoon drippings over. Add another 1/2 cup of broth and remaining salt and pepper. Cover and continue cooking until vegetables and meat are tender. Remove meat and vegetables to platter and cover with foil. Let meat stand 15 minutes before slicing, and slice against grain. Makes 8 servings.

**For gravy:** Add 3 cups beef broth to drippings in pan and stir well. Combine 2 tablespoons cornstarch with 2 tablespoons water and mix until smooth. Stir into gravy until mixture is smooth and bring to a boil. Cook until gravy is thickened.

# Sukiyaki

*This is a very easy Japanese-American dish that guests were usually not expecting to find on our small island!*

### INGREDIENTS:

2 tablespoons vegetable oil
2 pounds round steak, sliced into 2 inch strips
1 teaspoon garlic powder
1 teaspoon ground black pepper
1 pound white mushrooms, sliced thin
10 scallions, trimmed and cut into one inch pieces
6 ribs celery, sliced on the diagonal
2 cans bamboo shoots, drained
6 tablespoons water
1/3 cup soy sauce
1 cup chicken broth
1 package (about 1 pound) raw cleaned spinach leaves
3 cups cooked white rice

### DIRECTIONS:

In a large heavy skillet or frying pan, heat the oil over medium high heat and add the meat. Season with garlic powder and pepper and brown the pieces, stirring to cook evenly. Add remaining ingredients except spinach and rice and stir well. Reduce heat to medium low and simmer, uncovered, about 10 -12 minutes, until vegetables are just tender. Taste and adjust seasonings to suit taste, adding more soy sauce if desired. Add spinach and stir until wilted and heated through, but not overcooked. Remove from heat and serve with hot, fluffy white rice.

*Sukiyaki became popular in America during the late 1950s and early 1960s and is one many readers may not be old enough to remember-or ever heard of in Cayman, now that Asian fusion cuisine has become so available-and sophisticated. Simple sukiyaki was considered an exotic dish decades ago, when Chun King was "gourmet" Chinese fare for the home cook of the 1960s. Pepper steak is a close relative, and one enjoyed widely in the Caribbean today.*

# Swiss Steak

*This is an American dish, not a Swiss one. I found the recipe in a magazine that was very popular in the 1960s and added my own touches to make a creamier sauce. You could use turtle steak if you wanted, and make it even better.*

### INGREDIENTS:
3 pounds round steak, about 2 inches thick
½ cup flour
1/2 teaspoons salt
1/4 teaspoon black pepper
¼ teaspoon paprika
1/2 cup vegetable oil
2 large onions, sliced thin
1 10-3/4 ounce can condensed ream of mushroom soup
2 cups canned stewed tomatoes
Salt and black pepper to taste

### DIRECTIONS:
Cut off any excess fat from meat. Combine flour, salt, pepper and paprika and blend well. Place meat on a cutting board or other hard surface covered with plastic wrap. Sprinkle one side with half the flour and use a meat mallet to pound flour into meat. Turn meat over and repeat steps with remaining seasoned flour.

Heat the oil over medium high heat in a Dutch oven or large heavy skillet and cook onions until turning brown. Remove onions from pan and add the meat. Brown meat well on both sides, about 4 minutes per side. Reduce heat to low. Top meat with cooked onions, and pour in mushroom soup and tomatoes. Stir lightly to blend sauce in pan. Cover and simmer slowly over low heat 2 1/2 to 3 hours or until meat is fork tender. Check pan from time to time and a little water if necessary so there is enough cooking sauce. Add more salt or pepper to taste if desired. This is good served with hot mashed potatoes. Makes 8-10 servings and any leftovers taste very good the next day.

# Pepper Steak

*Paprika gives a nice boost to this recipe, but be sure your spice is fresh. You will be able to tell if it is rancid by the sharp "off" smell. Pepper steak is delicious served over hot white rice.*

**INGREDIENTS:**
2 pounds round steak
2 tablespoons sweet paprika
¼ cup butter or margarine
1 large onion, halved and sliced thin
4 cloves garlic, chopped
2 teaspoons seasoned salt
1 teaspoon black pepper
2 cups beef broth
2 medium green peppers, cut into ½ inch strips
1- 14.5 ounce can tomatoes, chopped
¼ cup soy sauce
2 tablespoons cornstarch
2 tablespoons water

**DIRECTIONS:**
Use a heavy meat mallet and pound the round steak until ¼ inch thick, then cut into strips about 2 inches long. Sprinkle meat with paprika and set aside while preparing other ingredients.

In a large heavy skillet or Dutch oven, melt the butter or margarine over medium high heat. Brown the meat, turning, until browned on all sides, then add the onion, garlic, seasoned salt and pepper and stir. Add the broth. Reduce heat to medium low and cover; simmer for 45 minutes or until meat is tender. Add the green pepper and tomatoes and stir. Cover and cook 5 minutes longer. Combine the cornstarch, soy sauce and water and mix until smooth, then stir into the pepper steak mixture. Cook, stirring frequently, until sauce is thickened, about 2 minutes. Makes 6- 8 servings.

## A Little Italy in East End

I used to make these dishes often at the Club and they were always a hit, not just with hotel guests. Local people used to come too when they heard Lasagna was on the menu. Back then, these recipes weren't familiar to most Caymanians and were new and exciting to me too. In those days, there were no Italian restaurants in Cayman like there are today, and stores weren't stocked with so many frozen convenience foods. Today you can buy frozen family size lasagna to microwave, so this may not seem special now. But my homemade Italian dishes were a first at the time!

# Cleo's Cayman Lasagna

*My recipe is different from most because I used different cheeses. As always, you can adjust the spices to suit your own taste.*

### INGREDIENTS:
1- 8 ounce box lasagna noodles
2 tablespoons olive oil
1 pound ground beef
2 cloves garlic, minced
1- 6 ounce can tomato paste
2-1/2 cups crushed tomatoes
   (1 pound, 4 ounce can)

1 teaspoon salt
¾ teaspoon black pepper
½ teaspoon oregano
1-1/2 cups grated or shredded
   Swiss cheese
1 -12 ounce container cottage
   cheese, mashed
Grated parmesan cheese

### DIRECTIONS:
Boil the noodles in salted water according to package directions, until firm tender but not too soft. Drain and set aside.

**Preheat oven to 350 F.**
Make the sauce: in large heavy skillet or Dutch oven, heat oil over medium high heat until hot, then add the beef and garlic and brown well. Stir in the tomato paste until mixed well and then add the crushed tomatoes and seasonings. Bring to a boil, then reduce heat to medium low, cover and simmer for 20 -30 minutes, stirring occasionally, to let flavors develop.

Spray an 11 x 7 inch baking dish with Pam and place a layer of noodles on the bottom, sprinkle with some of the grated cheese, then top with some of the cottage cheese and meat sauce. Repeat layers this way, ending with meat sauce on top. Top with remaining Swiss cheese. Bake at 350 for 20 -30 minutes, until bubbling and cheese on top is browned. Let cool 15 minutes to set, then cut into squares, using a spatula to remove from the pan. Serve with grated parmesan cheese on the side. Makes 6 – 8 servings.

# Spaghetti with Meat Balls

*This was another favorite dish that is not difficult to make. I wonder how many people make it at home today? It tastes even better the next day, if you have any leftovers.*

**MEATBALLS:**
2 cloves garlic, minced
1 teaspoon oregano
2-1/2 teaspoons salt
1 teaspoon ground black pepper
2 cups bread crumbs
1 cup grated parmesan cheese
1 cup milk
3 large eggs, beaten
1-1/2 pounds ground pork
1-1/2 pounds ground beef

**SAUCE:**
1/3 cup olive oil
4 cloves garlic, minced
1 cup chopped onion
4 large (1 pound 4 ounce) cans whole
   tomatoes, crushed or pureed
   in blender
2 – 6 ounce cans tomato paste
1 - 15 ounce cans tomato sauce
1-1/2 cups water
½ cup red wine
2 teaspoons basil
2 tablespoons minced parsley
   (fresh is best)
1 tablespoon salt
1 teaspoon ground black pepper
Spaghetti or other pasta, cooked

**DIRECTIONS:**

Make the meatballs: In large bowl, combine all ingredients except beef and pork and stir well, then crumble in meats and mix just until combined. Shape mixture into 1-inch balls (or desired size). In large heavy skillet, heat 3 tablespoons olive oil or fat over medium high heat and brown meatballs on all sides, draining off excess fat as it accumulates. Set cooked meatballs aside and cover with foil to keep warm. (You can bake the meatballs in a foil lined baking pan at 350 for 30 minutes, instead of frying, if you want.)

Make the sauce: In a large saucepan or Dutch oven, heat the olive oil until hot and sauté the onion and garlic over medium heat until soft. Gradually stir in the remaining ingredients until mixed and bring to a boil. Stir again, then reduce heat to low, cover and simmer, stirring occasionally for at least an hour. About 30 minutes before sauce is ready, add the meatballs and continue cooking. Just before serving, cook the spaghetti or desired pasta and drain. Spoon sauce with meatballs over hot pasta, and top with grated parmesan cheese if desired. Makes 8-12 servings.

# Delicious Chicken Dishes

# Curried Chicken

*This is still a favorite local dish today. Some people say the English brought curry to Cayman, because they remember it being served in restaurants in George Town that the English liked. But I believe it came over from Jamaica years ago. My curry has rich flavor, but it's not very hot, like many Indian curry dishes. You should use good quality curry powder with a fragrant aroma-stale spice will ruin this recipe. You can use more curry powder, if you like.*

### INGREDIENTS:
1 -3-4 pound frying chicken, cut into 12 pieces
Salt and black pepper
2 tablespoons vegetable oil
1 medium onion, chopped
1 small sweet green pepper, chopped
3 tablespoons curry powder
1 teaspoon salt
1 teaspoon black pepper
2 Irish potatoes, peeled and cut into pieces
Chicken broth

### DIRECTIONS:
Wash the chicken in cold water and vinegar and pat dry. Season all over with salt and pepper. Place the oil in a large heavy skillet or Dutch oven, and heat over medium high heat. Add all ingredients except potatoes and stir, turning until chicken and vegetables are evenly mixed with curry powder. Reduce heat to medium low and cover tightly. Let the chicken steam for 30 minutes, then remove cover and turn pieces. Add the potatoes. If the chicken and vegetables haven't released enough liquid to cook evenly, add ¾ - 1 cup chicken broth and continue cooking until chicken and potatoes are tender. Or, if you end up with thin gravy and need to thicken mix 1 tablespoon of cornstarch or flour with 2 tablespoons water and add to sauce, stirring well. Cook over medium heat 3- 4 minutes longer, until gravy is thickened.

# Cleo's Chicken & Dumplings

*This is how I made this Southern American dish, and it's different from any you've seen before. "Steaming" the chicken instead of boiling gives it a richer flavor. Cayman-style chicken 'n dumplins is a different dish. It is more like brown stew chicken with the firm flour dumplings. These are soft, rich and fluffy.*

### INGREDIENTS:
1 -3-1/2 to 4 pound frying chicken, cut into 12 pieces
1 teaspoon salt
1 teaspoon ground black pepper
1 tablespoon Kitchen bouquet
2 tablespoons vegetable oil
1 large yellow onion, peeled, quartered and sliced
2 - 10.5 ounce cans condensed cream of mushroom or cream of chicken soup
2 cups water

### DUMPLINGS:
1-1/2 cups flour
2 teaspoons baking powder
½ teaspoon salt
2 teaspoons sugar
1-1/2 tablespoons Crisco or other solid shortening
¾ cup milk

### DIRECTIONS:
Wash chicken pieces thoroughly in lime juice, vinegar and cold water. Pat dry and sprinkle with salt and pepper and Kitchen Bouquet. Heat oil in 5 quart Dutch oven over medium heat and add onions and stir. Place chicken pieces on top. Cover tightly; reduce heat to medium low and cook (we call this steaming) for 30 minutes. Remove cover and add soup and water and stir to blend until smooth -- make sure nothing is sticking to bottom of pan. Reduce heat to low, cover and cook over low heat for 30 minutes, until chicken is almost fork tender.

Make the dumplings: In medium bowl, mix together dry ingredients and blend well. Blend in the shortening until it is crumbly, then use a wooden spoon to mix in milk until a soft dough forms. Uncover chicken and drop dough, a large tablespoon at a time, onto hot chicken. Cook uncovered 15 minutes, then cover and cook another 20 minutes, until fluffy and done.

Taste the sauce and adjust gravy seasonings if desired, adding more black pepper and a pinch of chicken bouillon granules if desired.

# Chicken Paprika

This is a Hungarian recipe that I read in a magazine in the 1960s. Be sure your paprika hasn't gone off--dry spices like paprika can go rancid quickly in the heat and humidity of an island kitchen. Storing your spices in tightly closed containers in the refrigerator will help keep them fresh longer. If you can afford it or find it, use Hungarian or other good quality paprika. And you can use more if you want more flavor. If you don't use any hot paprika, then you might want to add a few slivers of country (Scotch Bonnet) pepper or a teaspoon of pepper sauce. This recipe should have a little bite to it.

### INGREDIENTS:
1- 3 pound frying chicken, cut into 12 serving pieces
Salt and black pepper
5 tablespoons vegetable oil
2 medium yellow onions, chopped
1 small green sweet pepper, seeded and chopped
2 cloves garlic, chopped fine
¼ -cup mild or sweet paprika + 2 tablespoons hot paprika
2 tablespoons cognac or brandy (Optional but traditional recipes call for it)
1 cup chicken broth
½ cup sour cream

### DIRECTIONS:
Wash chicken pieces with vinegar or lime and cold water and pat dry. Season with salt and pepper. In a large (5 quart) Dutch Oven, heat the oil until hot over medium high heat and brown the chicken about 3 minutes on each side (a few pieces at a time so the oil stays hot). Remove chicken to a plate and cover with foil. Reduce heat to medium and add the onions and green pepper and cook until turning soft, stirring often. Add the garlic, stirring well, and cook another minute, stirring several times so it doesn't scorch. Reduce heat to low, sprinkle the paprika over the mixture and stir well, and continue stirring while you cook another minute. Add the cognac or brandy, stir well, then add the chicken pieces and chicken broth and stir well.

Increase heat to high until mixture comes to a boil, stirring several times, then reduce heat to low, cover and simmer for an hour until chicken is fork tender. Remove chicken to a plate and cover with foil. Bring the sauce in the pot back to a boil, stirring several times, then reduce heat to medium and simmer until sauce has reduced and thickened, about 10 minutes. Remove from heat and stir in the sour cream until blended, then heat gently, over low heat, until hot-do not allow to boil. Add more salt and black pepper to taste, then pour over chicken and serve right away. This dish does not reheat well because the cream will break down.

# Cleo's Chicken in Orange Sauce

*I don't think anyone in East End had ever tasted a recipe like this before I served it at the Club, and everyone loved it. Fresh orange juice makes all the difference in this recipe, but you can use any kind except canned, which gives an "off" flavor.*

*INGREDIENTS:*
1 -3-1/2 -4 pound frying chicken, cut into 12 pieces
3 tablespoons vegetable oil
1 teaspoon salt
1 teaspoon ground black pepper
1 teaspoon poultry seasoning

*ORANGE SAUCE:*
2 cups water
2 tablespoons cornstarch
2 cups orange juice
1 tablespoon butter, melted

*DIRECTIONS:*
Preheat oven to 350 F. Line a 12 x 15 baking pan with aluminum foil. Wash the chicken pieces thoroughly with lime juice or vinegar and cold water. Pat dry. Place chicken in large bowl and sprinkle with vegetable oil, then salt, pepper and poultry seasoning and toss or rub with fingers so all pieces are coated. Place chicken in prepared baking pan and cover with foil. Bake at 350 F for 20 minutes.

While chicken is baking, make the orange sauce. In a medium saucepan, blend the cornstarch with ¼ cup water until smooth, then add remaining water, orange juice and butter. Blend well. Cook over medium heat, stirring frequently, until sauce begins to thicken. Remove chicken from oven and pour sauce evenly over pieces. Return chicken to oven, uncovered, and bake another 30 minutes until chicken is nicely browned and glazed and tender. Makes 6 -8 servings.

# Chinese Fried Chicken

*This dish was always a hit with guests, many of whom tasted fresh ginger for the first time. I don't think it's really very Chinese, but more Caribbean.*

### INGREDIENTS:
1 3-pound frying chicken, cut into 12 pieces
1 teaspoon salt
1 teaspoon ground black pepper
1 tablespoon soy sauce
Peanut oil
¼ cup soy sauce
6 tablespoons water
2 tablespoons fresh peeled shredded ginger
6 large scallions, chopped (white and green parts)
¼ cup sherry or sweet white wine
Chopped fresh parsley (for garnish)

### DIRECTIONS:
Wash the chicken well in vinegar or lime juice and water. Pat dry. Place pieces in large bowl and sprinkle with salt and pepper and soy sauce. Rub pieces well with these seasonings. Pour peanut oil to ½ inch deep in a large heavy skillet or Dutch oven and heat over medium high heat until oil sizzles (is very hot, about 375). Add chicken, a few pieces at a time, so oil stays hot and they fry evenly. Reduce heat to medium and fry slowly, turning pieces occasionally. When all chicken pieces are nicely browned, mix together the remaining ingredients except parsley and pour over chicken; stir gently to distribute ingredients and turn chicken to coat with sauce. Cover, reduce heat to low and cook another 25-30 minutes. Remove chicken to serving plates, spoon with remaining sauce in pan and sprinkle with parsley.

# Cleo's Fried Chicken

*The secret to good fried chicken is freshening the chicken by soaking in vinegar and water, then seasoning the pieces. Another secret is keeping the oil hot enough to fry the pieces properly. It must be very hot, but not smoking, and don't crowd the chicken! Cook in small batches to keep the oil hot. One 3- pound frying chicken will make eight pieces, but I can't tell you how many servings. The way people love fried chicken, it could be only two!*

**INGREDIENTS:**
1-3 pound frying chicken, cut up
¼ cup cider vinegar
2 tablespoons salt
Cold water

Salt and black pepper
1-1/2 cups flour
1 teaspoon salt

1-1/2 teaspoons Season All
   or seasoned salt
1/2 teaspoon black pepper
½ teaspoon garlic salt
1 teaspoon paprika
1/2 teaspoon poultry seasoning
* 1 teaspoon red (cayenne) pepper
   (optional, only if you like hot pepper!)
Corn or peanut oil for frying

**DIRECTIONS:**
Wash the chicken in cold water, then cut into eight pieces. Leave the skin on, but cut away any excess fat. Place in a large glass or plastic bowl and cover with water, then add the vinegar and salt and stir to distribute evenly. Cover with wax paper and let stand for 30 minutes to an hour. Remove chicken from water and drain well. Pat dry with paper towels and sprinkle pieces all over evenly with salt and black pepper. Set aside for 15 minutes.

In a large mixing bowl, mix together the flour and dry spices and blend well. Dredge chicken pieces, one at a time, in flour mixture and shake off excess flour. Lay on wax paper while preparing pan. (You can also put the flour and spices in a heavy Ziplock bag instead, and shake the individual chicken pieces to coat.)

In a heavy 12-inch skillet or Dutch oven, heat 2 inches of oil (or enough Crisco to measure this) to very hot, 375 degrees. Fry chicken in batches, without crowding about 10 minutes on each side. If pierced, any juices should run clear. Drain chicken on paper towels on top of paper bag. If cooking large batches, heat oven to 200 F and keep chicken warm on paper-towel lined baking sheet.

Some still prefer to use solid Crisco vegetable shortening for frying, but you need enough to measure 2 inches deep in the skillet when it melts. Corn oil and peanut oil are best for frying food because they take high heat without smoking or burning.

# Chicken and Oyster Pie

*This is not an old Caymanian recipe. We have mangrove oysters in Cayman, but not ones you eat. We have to import them and once in awhile the Club would get in fresh oysters and I made this recipe I found in a cookbook. This is a very simple recipe and you can add more seasoning, such as a little country pepper, a few dashes of pepper sauce, chopped parsley, or onion flakes if you want.*

## INGREDIENTS:

¼ cup butter
¼ cup flour
½ teaspoon salt
1/8 teaspoon ground black pepper
¼ teaspoon nutmeg (if desired)
2-1/2 cups cream (evaporated milk) or whole milk

3 cups cooked chicken, cut into small cubes
1 pint fresh oysters (shelled, cleaned and drained)
2 tablespoons butter, cut into small pieces
½ teaspoon salt
¼ teaspoon ground black pepper

Flaky Crust for 9-inch pie (one crust)

## DIRECTIONS:

Butter a 3-quart casserole or baking dish. Make a white sauce from the first five (or six if using nutmeg) ingredients. In a medium skillet or saucepan, melt the butter over medium heat until bubbling. Sprinkle the flour, salt and pepper over butter and stir until blended. Reduce heat to low and cook, stirring frequently, 2-3 minutes. Remove from heat and gradually stir in milk or cream, stirring constantly-use a wire whisk if necessary to beat until mixture is free of lumps. Return to heat and cook and stir until sauce is smooth and thickened. If too thick, add a little more cream or milk to desired thickness. Sauce should not be too thin for this recipe.

Preheat oven to 375 F. Combine the chicken and oysters in the buttered casserole and dot evenly with the butter. Sprinkle evenly with salt and pepper, then pour the white sauce over. Cover the mixture with the pie crust, seal or crimp the edges all around and prick top with a fork in several places to let steam escape. Bake on rack in center of oven for 35-40 minutes, until crust is golden and filling bubbly and hot.

Remove from oven and let cool 10 minutes before serving.

# Barbecue & Peppers

Well, I hope you aren't disappointed. I just did not do barbecue. I'm allergic to all kinds of smoke so there isn't a barbecue chapter in my book. When I cooked for guests, we had a barbecue outside once a week. I would prepare the meat and sauces but I always let another one of the staff do the barbequing. I did make barbecue chicken and ribs in the oven during the week.

Another thing I didn't cook was jerk chicken or pork. That's a Jamaican thing and only became popular in Cayman in the last 20 years. Jerk wasn't heard of out here when I was in charge of the Tortuga Club kitchen. It would have been too highly spiced for most guests of that time. Today, it seems everyone like things hot, hot, hot! I see guests reaching for pepper sauce to use on everything! I can't understand it.

I was very careful with my guests. Back then, hot pepper was an insult. Foreign guests had never tasted anything like our peppers and it would have been a shock to most of them. So I didn't cook with pepper, but sometimes we offered pepper sauce if guests asked for it.

Now I believe that too much pepper is bad for you, especially men. It can do bad things to your insides. I don't care what they say about it. But this is a favorite seasoning on Caymanian tables and I wanted to include the recipe for those who like their pepper.

# Old Time Cayman Pepper Sauce

*This is how Caymanians made pepper sauce years ago, and you spoon out a little of the hot vinegar to add to soups or season your food. Some eat the peppers and vegetables too!*

**INGREDIENTS:**
2 cups fresh Cayman peppers (Scotch Bonnet)
1 small yellow onion, thinly sliced in rings
1-2 cups cider vinegar (enough to fill jar)
1 teaspoon salt

**DIRECTIONS:**
Wash and drain the peppers before slicing into rings. Have a large clean glass jar-make sure it is clean-waiting. Fill alternately with slices of Scotch bonnet peppers of different colors (green, red and orange, including seeds) and sliced onion. Add of salt. In a small saucepan, heat enough vinegar until boiling, then remove from heat and pour carefully into jar over peppers. Seal jar tightly and store for two weeks, away from light. This improves as it ages.

**Variations:** Some leave the peppers whole, but pierced instead of slicing. Some like to add slices of carrot and garlic, or whole allspice berries as well.

## What are Seasoning Peppers?

*In Cayman, our local "seasoning peppers" are small, flatter relatives of the Scotch Bonnet and have much of the same flavor without the heat. They are unique to Cayman and easy to find in Grand Cayman's local supermarket produce sections, but not available overseas.*

# Cleo's Famous Homemade Pies

Pies were one of my favorite things to make: my Key Lime and Coconut Cream Pies were the most "famous". The one kind I did not make was chocolate and to this day I don't really remember why. Maybe it was because I don't eat chocolate myself. I often made my crusts from breadcrumbs instead of pastry, which was different and that recipe is below.

It grieves me when I see the way people cook today. Why do they use frozen crusts instead of learning to make a good pie crust from scratch? It isn't hard and a good crust is as important to a pie as the filling. And a bad crust ruins a good pie. You might as well just eat the filling from a bowl with a spoon!

# Old Time Flaky Pie Crust

*Some still like to have a pie with a flaky crust. Lard was the secret ingredient in old time pie crusts. It makes the flakiest, tenderest crust you could imagine. Since that's a word that frightens away bakers today, this recipe includes the measurements for both lard and Crisco. And remember: you don't knead pie crust like you do biscuit dough. You gather it into a ball-too much handling will make a tough crust.*

**For single-crust 8 or 9 inch pie**
**(For two-crust pie, double the measurements)**

| | |
|---|---|
| *INGREDIENTS:* | Or |
| 1 cup sifted flour | 1 cup plus 2 tablespoons sifted flour |
| 1/4 teaspoon salt | ¼ teaspoon salt |
| 1/3 cup lard | 1/3 cup Crisco or solid vegetable |
| 2-3 tablespoons cold water |    shortening |
| | 2-3 tablespoons cold water |

*DIRECTIONS:*

In a medium mixing bowl, whisk together the sifted flour and salt. Using a pastry blender, two knives or your fingertips, work in the lard or shortening until mixture resembles crumbs the size of peas. Sprinkle water over, a tablespoon at a time, and mix lightly with a fork after each addition, adding just enough water so dough holds together and pulls away from side of bowl-do not use more water than needed.

Handle dough gently! Form dough into a ball and turn out onto lightly floured surface lined with wax paper (this will make transferring the crust to the pie pan easier). Use as little flour in rolling as possible, as additional flour toughens the crust.

If using two-crust recipe, divide dough in half. Flour hands, flatten ball of dough, then roll out with lightly floured rolling pin to just under 1/8 inch thick-you can use a top layer of floured wax paper. Keep rounding out the edge of the pastry, pressing broken edges back together. Roll crust out about 1 inch larger all around than the outer rim of pie pan. Carefully transfer the rolled pastry to the pie pan, and remove wax paper, if using.

**Now this is important:** gently ease the pastry loosely into pie pan, being careful not to pull or stretch! This will cause the crust to shrink during baking.  Gently press dough into pan, smoothing and patching any thin spots with overhanging dough from rim until pie shell is even as possible.

**For pie baked with filling:** Trim pastry ½ inch beyond edge of pie pan and crimp edges and flute as desired, so that edge is even with pan, but do not prick the crust! Fill and proceed with recipe or wrap tightly with plastic wrap and chill until ready to use.

**For baked pie shell:** Preheat oven to 425F. Follow directions above, but prick bottom and sides with fork at half-inch intervals. Line crust with a 12-inch square piece of parchment paper or aluminum foil covered with four tablespoons of dried beans (or if you have real pie weights, use them). Place in the upper third of the oven and bake for 5-6 minutes, then remove foil and beans, and bake an additional 8-10 minutes until light golden brown. After removing paper or foil, check crust through oven window several times-if crust is puffing or swelling, open oven and press gently with tines of fork. Remove from oven and place on wire rack to cook completely before filling.

**For partially baked crust** (tip-this is the best crust for custard pies) Follow directions for baked pie shell, but remove foil and beans after 6 minutes and bake only an additional 4 minutes. Remove from oven and place on wire rack to cook completely before filling.

Now, let's get on with the pies!

- Handle dough as little as possible. When you can gather dough into ball without crumbling, stop adding water and stop handling.
- Rolling crust out between pieces of wax paper helps cut down the extra flour needed
- Use as little flour as possible when handling and rolling—it makes the dough tough instead of flaky and tender
- Use pie weights, dried beans or foil to weight an unfilled crust during baking
- For fruit pies, brush bottom crust lightly with egg white or melted butter before baking to prevent from getting soggy
- Putting hot filling into unbaked pie crust helps prevent sogginess too
- Cut slits in top crust of filled pies to allow steam to escape
- Brush top crust lightly with milk or cream and sprinkle with sugar before baking
- Pies should begin in hot oven, 425 for 15 minutes, then lower heat to 350 for remainder (40-50 minutes)
- For fruit filled pies, top should be golden brown and filling should be bubbling with a little appearing through slits in top when done.

# Cleo's Cayman Lime Pie

*This was one of my most famous pies. I still hear from people today who ask for a copy of my lime pie recipe! No matter what others say about pale yellow being the true color of real key lime pie, I believe that lime pie should be green, and adding a few drops of green food coloring is important. Lemon pie is yellow. My foreign guests expected to see a little green in their Cayman lime pie!*

**CRUST:**
2 cups dry bread crumbs
3 tablespoons margarine
   or butter, melted
1/2 teaspoon cinnamon
1 tablespoon brown sugar

**FILLING:**
4 tablespoons unflavored gelatin
1-1/2 cups sugar
¼ teaspoon salt
4 large egg yolks, beaten
½ cup fresh lime juice
   (key lime is best)
¾ cup water
4 drops green food coloring
1 cup heavy cream, whipped
   until soft peaks form
4 egg whites
1 tablespoon sugar

## DIRECTIONS:

Preheat oven to 350 F. Combine the ingredients for the crust in a medium mixing bowl and blend well. Press into a 9 inch pie dish. Bake crust about 10 minutes, until set.

In a large saucepan, mix together the gelatin, sugar, salt to blend, then stir in the egg yolks, lime juice, and water. Over medium high heat, bring to a boil, then reduce heat to medium low. Cook, stirring constantly, until filling has thickened. Remove from heat, stir in food coloring; spoon into a bowl and chill until set, about 2 hours. To finish pie, beat egg whites with sugar until stiff peaks form, then fold into whipped cream, very lightly, just to blend. Gently fold the cream mixture into the lime gelatin filling and spoon into crust. Chill pie two hours at least before serving. Top each slice with additional whipped cream if desired.

# Cleo's Coconut Cream Pie

*Please use fresh coconut if possible. It makes all the difference in the world. When I made this pie, I used a half-hard coconut. Not a green one, and not a hard brown one, but one whose meat had a thin, pale brown skin that was easy to peel off, and the meat tender and sweet. I shredded the coconut by scraping the peeled pieces on a box grater in one direction only, not up and down.*

1 9-inch baked pie crust

**FILLING:**
1-1/2 cups sugar
¼ teaspoon salt
¼ cup cornstarch
1-1/2 cups cream (evaporated milk)
3 large egg yolks, beaten
3 tablespoons butter, softened
1 teaspoon vanilla
1 cup shredded fresh coconut
2 tablespoons shredded coconut for topping

**DIRECTIONS:**

**Make filling:** In a medium saucepan, mix together sugar, salt and cornstarch. Use a wire whisk instead of a spoon for this recipe. Over medium low heat, gradually whisk in evaporated milk and cook, stirring constantly, until mixture thickens and comes to a full boil, about 4-5 minutes. Continue boiling and stirring for 1 minute longer, then remove from heat. Put the beaten egg yolks in a small bowl and measure out ½ cup of the milk custard and whisk into the eggs, then whisk this into custard in saucepan. Return to heat and cook, stirring constantly, until custard returns to a full boil, about 4 minutes longer. Remove from heat and gently but evenly blend in the butter and vanilla, then stir in the coconut. Let cool ten minutes.

Spoon the custard evenly into pie crust. Cover pie firmly with plastic wrap and chill at least 4 hours. Serve topped with sweetened whipped cream or whipped topping, sprinkled with remaining coconut.

# Miss Cleo's Sweet Breadcrumb Crust for Pies and Desserts

*This is enough for a one-crust 9-inch pie or a 9 inch square pan (bottom) or to line the bottom of a 9-inch springform pan for cheesecake.*

### INGREDIENTS:
1-1/2 cups dry breadcrumbs
4 tablespoons (1/4 cup) butter, melted
2 tablespoons white sugar
1 tablespoon brown sugar
¼ teaspoon cinnamon

### DIRECTIONS:
Preheat oven to 350F. Combine the crumbs, butter, sugars and cinnamon in a medium bowl and blend gently. Spoon into a 9-inch pie pan or baking dish and use the back of a spoon to press firmly against bottom and sides of the pan. Bake 8 -10 minutes, but do not allow to over brown! Cool completely before filling.

# Banana Cream Pie

*What I see in the frozen food sections of stores today as banana cream pie is not the real thing. You can't make custard cream with any kind of artificial banana flavoring —it tastes awful. The bananas must be ripe, but not overripe and sliced thin. And the custard should be spooned over the bananas while still hot, so it will draw out the flavor of the bananas. I liked to make my pies with a baked pastry crust, but you can use the vanilla wafer crust too.*

1 -9 inch baked pie crust or

**INGREDIENTS:**
**VANILLA WAFER CRUST:**
1-1/4 cups crushed vanilla wafer crumbs
¼ cup butter or margarine, melted
1 tablespoon sugar
¼ teaspoon cinnamon

**FILLING:**
2/3 cup sugar
4 tablespoons cornstarch
¼ teaspoon nutmeg
1/2 teaspoon salt
3 cups whole milk
4 large egg yolks, lightly beaten
2 tablespoons butter or margarine, softened
1 tablespoon vanilla extract
3 medium ripe bananas
Additional banana slices for top garnish, if desired

**TOPPING:**
1 cup chilled whipping cream
2 tablespoons confectioner's sugar

**DIRECTIONS:**
Preheat oven to 375 F. Make the crust: In a small bowl, blend all ingredients with a fork until moistened. Press mixture evenly into a 9-inch pie pan, leaving a small edge at the top. Bake 10 minutes, until just turning light golden brown. Cool crust completely before filling.

**Make filling:** In a medium saucepan, mix together sugar, cornstarch, nutmeg and salt. Use a wire whisk instead of a spoon for this recipe. Over medium heat, gradually whisk in milk, and cook, stirring constantly, until mixture thickens and comes to a full boil, about 4-5 minutes. Continue boiling and stirring for 1 minute longer, then remove from heat. Put the beaten egg yolks in a small bowl and measure out 1 cup of the milk custard and whisk into the eggs, then whisk this into custard in saucepan. Return to heat and cook, stirring constantly until custard returns to a boil and is very thick, about 5- 6 minutes longer. Remove from heat and gently blend in the butter and vanilla until smooth.

Peel the bananas and slice thin crosswise (round slices). Layer half the bananas over the bottom of the baked crust and stir the rest into the hot custard. Then spoon the custard into crust evenly. You can arrange additional banana slices over top if you wish. Cover pie with plastic wrap. Refrigerate until completely chilled, at least 4 hours. Just before serving, combine whipping cream and sugar in small bowl and beat until soft peaks form. Swirl sweetened whipped cream over top and garnish with a few banana slices if desired.

# Lemon Meringue Pie

Not many people can be bothered to make this wonderful recipe anymore, with so many frozen pies available. It's just not the same. How can you freeze a meringue topping and expect it to taste good? Here in the humid tropical climate of Cayman, this pie is best served the same day. Meringue tends to "weep" in humid weather, so this kind of pie won't be as attractive when served as leftovers.

Grated lemon peel is what gives the lemon flavor boost-use more if you want a more tart taste. Another tip: separate the eggs while they are cold, but let them reach room temperature before beating the whites. And the bowl and beaters must be very clean and grease-free or the whites won't stiffen properly.

**1 baked 9 inch pie crust, cooled**

### INGREDIENTS:
1-1/2 cups sugar
5 tablespoons cornstarch
¼ teaspoon salt
1-1/2 cups water
3 large egg yolks, lightly beaten
3 tablespoons butter
1/4 cup lemon juice
1 tablespoon grated lemon peel

4 large egg whites
1/4 teaspoon cream of tartar or 1 teaspoon lemon juice
½ teaspoon vanilla
¼ cup sugar

### DIRECTIONS:
In a medium saucepan, whisk together sugar, cornstarch and salt until blended. Gradually add water, stirring until smooth. Over medium heat, cook mixture until it comes to a boil, stirring constantly, and continue cooking until mixture thickens, about 1 minute longer. Remove from heat. Gradually add half the hot mixture to yolks, stir well, then return egg mixture to saucepan, stirring constantly. Return to medium heat and cook, stirring constantly, another minute longer. Remove from heat and stir in butter, lemon juice and lemon zest, blending until smooth. Spoon evenly into baked pie shell.

Preheat oven to 400 F. In medium glass bowl, beat egg whites and cream of tarter on high speed for a minute, then gradually add vanilla and sugar, 1 tablespoon at a time, beating about 3-4 minutes, until stiff, glossy peaks form. Swirl meringue over hot pie filling, covering top and sealing pie at the edges. Bake 8-10 minutes or until peaks turn light golden brown. Remove pie from oven and cool on wire rack for 30 minutes before serving.

# Pineapple Pie

*No one makes this anymore and it is delicious. A recipe for fresh pineapple pie follows-but in the 1960s, this was an expensive luxury and canned pineapple made a fine pie. If you want, you can add ½ cup shredded coconut to the filling when you add the crushed pineapple.*

**1 baked 9 inch pie shell**

*FOR FILLING:*
**3 large egg yolks**
**1 cup sugar**
**½ cup cornstarch**
**½ cup water or coconut water (better!)**
**1 cup pineapple juice**
**3 tablespoons butter**
**1 tablespoon fresh lime juice**
**2 teaspoons grated lime peel**
**1-1/4 cups well-drained crushed pineapple**

*FOR MERINGUE:*
**3 large egg whites**
**¼ teaspoon lime juice**
**6 tablespoons sugar**
**½ teaspoon vanilla or rum flavoring**

*DIRECTIONS:*
In a small bowl, lightly beat the egg yolks. In large saucepan, whisk together the sugar and cornstarch. Gradually whisk in the water or coconut water and pineapple juice. Cook over medium heat, stirring constantly, until mixture thickens and comes to a boil, then continue cooking for 1 minute. Remove from heat and slowly stir half of the sugar mixture into the egg yolks. Blend well then stir the egg mixture into remaining sugar mixture in saucepan. Return to heat and bring to a low boil for one minute, stirring constantly. Remove from heat and stir in the butter, lime juice and peel, then slowly stir in the drained pineapple. Pour into the baked pie crust.

Preheat oven to 400 F. Make the meringue: In a medium bowl, beat the egg whites with the lime juice until frothy, then beat in the sugar, a little at a time, until whites form stiff, glossy peaks then add flavoring and beat another 30 seconds. Pile meringue onto hot pie filling and swirl gently and spread, sealing meringue onto the edge of the crust. Bake 8-10 minutes, until just golden brown.

# Fresh Caribbean Pineapple Pie

*Local farmers in East End and North Side now grow some sweet little pineapples, perfect for this recipe. Use only sweet, ripe pineapple. The rum is optional-you can use fresh lime juice instead if you don't like spirits.*

**Pastry for a 2-crust 9-inch pie crust, unbaked**

### INGREDIENTS:
6 cups fresh pineapple, cored, peeled and chopped into fine pieces
1 cup sugar
2 tablespoons dark rum or lime juice
1/2 cup brown sugar
½ cup flour
½ teaspoon ground cinnamon
1/4 teaspoon ground nutmeg
1 tablespoon butter or margarine

### DIRECTIONS:
Place pineapple in large glass or plastic bowl and sprinkle with 1 cup sugar and rum or lime juice and stir well. Cover and refrigerate at least 4 hours to draw the juices out. Drain pineapple, reserving ½ cup of the juice. Whisk together brown sugar, cornstarch, cinnamon and nutmeg in saucepan. Stir in the reserved pineapple juice and bring to a boil and cook, stirring constantly for 1 minute. Remove from heat and stir in butter. Spoon pineapple into pastry-lined 9-inch pie plate. Pour hot sugar mixture over pineapple. Trim overhanging edge of pastry to 1 inch from rim of plate.

Top pie with latticework crust, or solid crust pricked all over with fork. Fold trimmed edge of lower crust over ends of strips; seal and press with the flat side of a fork to flute.

It's best if you cover the crust edge with 3-inch strip of aluminum foil to prevent it from over browning, and remove foil during last 15 minutes of baking. Bake at 425 F until crust is golden brown and filling is bubbly, 35 to 45 minutes.

# Hawaiian Banana Pie

*Our sweet small Cayman apple bananas are especially delicious in this recipe.*

**1- 9 inch pie crust, unbaked (two crust recipe)**

### INGREDIENTS:
**6 cups sliced ripe bananas**
**¾ cup pineapple juice**
**¾ cup sugar**
**1 tablespoon flour**
**1-1/2 teaspoons cinnamon**
**1 tablespoon butter, cut into small pieces**

### DIRECTIONS:
Preheat oven to 400 F. Have the pie dish lined with bottom crust, and top crust rolled out and ready to use.

Place bananas in a small plastic or glass bowl and pour pineapple juice over. Soak bananas for 30 minutes, then drain off juice and save. Layer bananas in unbaked pie crust. Combine the sugar, flour and cinnamon and blend well. Sprinkle evenly over bananas. Measure 3 tablespoons of the reserved pineapple juice and pour evenly over bananas. Dot top with butter. Place the top crust over filling and cut slits in top to allow steam to escape. Bake at 400 for 40-45 minutes, or until crust is golden brown and filling is bubbling (seen through slit). Remove from oven and cool on wire rack an hour before serving.

# Cherry Banana Pie

*Years ago, canned cherries were the only ones available here. Today you'll find fresh and frozen Bing and other cherries in our supermarkets. But my original recipe calls for canned cherries —not maraschino cherries--and it is delicious just that way.*

**INGREDIENTS:**
1 -9 inch single crust pie crust, unbaked
3 cups sliced ripe bananas
3 cups tart pitted canned cherries, drained well
¾ cup sugar
1 teaspoon nutmeg
2 tablespoons flour
1-1/2 tablespoons butter, cut into small pieces

**DIRECTIONS:**
Preheat oven to 400 F. Combine sugar, nutmeg and flour and blend well. Place fruit in a medium bowl and sprinkle with sugar mixture. Toss lightly until mixed, then spoon into prepared crust and dot evenly with butter. Bake 35- 40 minutes, until filling is firm and crust is browned. Remove from oven and cool 30 minutes, but serve warm, with a dollop of whipped cream or whipped topping.

# Cayman Banana Coconut Custard Pie

**INGREDIENTS:**

1/2 cup flour
1 1/2 cups sugar
1/8 teaspoon salt
¼ teaspoon nutmeg
2 large eggs, lightly beaten
1-1/2 cups evaporated milk
½ cup water
1 tablespoon butter, softened
2 teaspoons vanilla extract-divided
6 ripe apple bananas
½ cup plus 2 tablespoons
   shredded
   coconut, lightly toasted
9" baked pie shell
1 cup whipping cream
1 tablespoon confectioner's sugar

**DIRECTIONS:**

Combine flour, sugar, salt, nutmeg and eggs in a medium saucepan. Beat with hand beater or wire whisk until well mixed. Combine milk and water and add to egg mixture, continue beating until smooth. Cook over medium heat until mixture thickens, stirring constantly, about 8 minutes.

Remove from heat. Stir in butter and 1 teaspoon vanilla into hot mixture, then stir in ½ cup coconut. Peel the bananas and slice thin crosswise (round slices). Layer half the bananas over the bottom of the baked crust and stir the rest into the hot custard. Then spoon the custard into crust evenly. You can arrange additional banana slices over top if you wish. Cover pie with plastic wrap. Refrigerate until completely chilled, at least 4 hours. Just before serving, combine whipping cream and sugar in small bowl and beat until soft peaks form. Swirl sweetened whipped cream over top and garnish with remaining 2 tablespoons toasted coconut.

# Cho-Cho Pie with Crumb Topping

*I used to make this pie for guests and then ask them what they thought the filling was made of. They always said "green apples!" I think cho-chos are an overrated little squash that take more work than they deserve to make tasty as a vegetable. But they do make a good apple substitute in pies!*

**1 - 9 inch unbaked pie crust**

**FILLING:**
4 cho-chos
1 cup water
3 allspice berries
1/2 cup brown sugar
½ cup white sugar
2 tablespoons lime juice
2 tablespoons cornstarch
½ teaspoon cinnamon

**CRUMB TOPPING:**
¼ cup margarine, cut into pieces
1 cup flour
½ cup brown sugar

**DIRECTIONS:**
Line a 9 inch pie pan with half the crust recipe. Peel and core the cho-chos, then slice into thin slices, about an inch long. Parboil the cho-chos in the water with allspice berries until just crisp tender-- do not allow them to get mushy. Remove cho-chos from water with slotted spoon and set aside to cool. Strain allspice from water. Mix together sugars, lime juice and cornstarch and blend well. Stir into cooking water and bring to a boil, then reduce heat to simmer and cook until mixture is reduced to a thick syrup. Remove from heat and cool.

Preheat oven to 375F. Arrange the cho-cho pieces in the crust, then pour the cooled syrup evenly over cho-chos and sprinkle with cinnamon. Mix the topping: combine all ingredients in a small bowl and using two knives or a pastry blender, mix until crumbly, or mixture has pea-sized crumbs. Sprinkle evenly over filling and bake for 35-40 minutes, until crust and topping are golden brown.

# Cakes, Desserts and Special Sweets

My desserts were always one of the highlights of dinner for guests at the Club. Many guests invited me to visit them overseas. I liked to surprise them by making their favorites in their homes. One time I went to visit friends in California and as soon as I got there, I asked them to take me to a store. I wanted to buy the ingredients for a Chocolate Supreme, which they loved. I didn't go on vacation to cook, but I loved cooking for my friends. Of all the recipes I have been asked for over the years, ones for my pies and desserts were requested most.

# Coconut Pound Cake

*Visitors always seemed to expect coconut desserts in the islands! My usual coconut cake was simple. I would make a simple white cake for dessert at the Club. I never put the coconut in the cake batter because it made it too crumbly. I sprinkled generous amount of grated coconut between the frosted layers and on the top and sides. Today's white cake mixes are good enough to use and I often used them myself. I am giving you this pound cake recipe instead, because it is from scratch and very nice for a party or celebration.*

*This is a delicious recipe that puts the coconut in the batter. It makes a rich cake that doesn't need frosting, and is also nice for breakfast. It is easy to make in a tube or bundt pan and keeps very well.*

### INGREDIENTS:
3 cups sifted flour, measured
   after sifting
1/2 teaspoon baking soda
¼ teaspoon salt
3 cups sugar
1-1/2 cups butter, at room
   temperature

6 large eggs at room temperature
1 cup sour cream
1 tablespoon coconut flavoring
   or extract
1 teaspoon almond flavoring
   or extract
2 cups freshly grated coconut

### DIRECTIONS:
Preheat oven to 325 F. Lightly grease and flour, or spray with Bakers Joy, a 10 inch tube pan or 12 cup bundt pan. In small mixing bowl, whisk together the flour, baking soda and salt. In large mixing bowl of an electric mixer, on high speed, cream the butter until light and almost like whipped cream. Slowly add the sugar, beating until smooth and light. On medium speed, add eggs, one at a time, beating well after each addition. On low speed, blend in the sour cream. Gradually add flour mixture, a half cup at a time, blending until smooth after each addition. Add the coconut and almond flavorings. Fold in grated coconut. Pour batter into prepared pan and bake for 1 hour and 15 minutes, or until wooden pick inserted in center comes out clean. Cool in pan for 15 minutes, then remove and cook completely on wire rack. Makes about 20 servings.

# Chocolate Supreme

*This was one of my most popular desserts. It was a good recipe for when things were scarce, as everything you needed could come from the pantry.*

**INGREDIENTS:**
4 tablespoons butter
2 cups flour
1 cup sugar
1 cup unsweetened cocoa
3 teaspoons baking powder
½ teaspoon salt
2 cups cream (evaporated milk)
1 cup light brown sugar
1 cup white sugar
½ cup unsweetened cocoa
3 cups boiling water

**DIRECTIONS:**
Preheat oven to 350 F. Place the butter in a 13 x 9 inch baking dish or casserole and place dish in oven until butter is melted. Remove from oven and make the cake batter. In a large mixing bowl, combine flour, sugar, cocoa, baking powder and salt and mix with a fork or wire whisk. Add the cream and mix well. Pour into the prepared baking dish. In a medium bowl, mix together the remaining sugars and cocoa and sprinkle evenly over the batter in the dish. Gradually pour the boiling water evenly over the batter. Do not mix! Bake at 350 F for 40-45 minutes. The cake will rise to the top and the bottom will be a rich, custardy chocolate sauce. Cool 15-20 minutes, but serve while warm. Use a spatula or pancake turner to cut slices of cake, then spoon the sauce from the pan over the cake.

# Cleo's Prize Lemon Cake

*This delicious and different recipe is similar to what was called Lemon Pudding Cake in the 1960s. The top is a layer of sponge cake over creamy lemon pudding. This is a large recipe that calls for a 10 x 15 inch (3 quart) baking dish, and an ideal dessert to bring to a party or family gathering.*

### INGREDIENTS:
3 cups sugar
¾ cup flour
¾ teaspoon salt
6 large egg yolks, beaten lightly
3 cups cream (evaporated milk)
8 tablespoons butter or margarine, melted
¾ cup lemon juice
2 tablespoons grated lemon peel
6 large egg whites

### DIRECTIONS:
Preheat oven to 350 F. Butter a large, 10 x 15 inch baking dish. Place dish in a larger roasting pan, one large enough to allow a hot water bath to come halfway up the side of the baking dish.

In a large mixing bowl, whisk together the sugar, flour and salt. In another large bowl, combine the beaten egg yolks, cream, melted butter, lemon juice and grated peel and blend until smooth. Pour into the sugar mixture and blend well. Beat the egg whites until stiff peaks form, then gently fold into the lemon mixture-do not stir, fold in just until blended. Spoon the batter into the prepared baking dish and place dish in larger roasting pan. Pour hot water into pan, halfway up the sides of the baking dish and bake for 45-50 minutes. The bottom will be a soft pudding and the top should be light golden brown-remove from oven and cool 15 minutes before serving. Serve warm or cold (warm is better!) with sweetened whipped cream if desired.

# Cleo's Bread Pudding

This was one of my most popular recipes and even today returning guests and island friends ask for it. This is an easy dessert to make, but most people today make bread pudding too firm! It is not supposed to be like heavy cake, it should be custardy. And don't soak the raisins or they will store too much liquid and the pudding won't come out right. You use a spoon to serve my bread pudding; you don't cut it with a knife. I don't know how people eat some of the things served as bread pudding today. Now I know Cubans and some Hondurans like theirs that way, but not Caymanians. I am also giving you a recipe for a large steam-table sized pan pudding, which is perfect for church functions, parties and dinners.

## INGREDIENTS:
**8 slices white bread or 8 small dinner rolls**
**3 cups cream (evaporated milk)**
**6 large eggs, beaten**
**¼ cup melted butter**
**1-1/2 cups sugar**
**1/4 teaspoon salt**
**1 teaspoon cinnamon**
**1/4 teaspoon nutmeg**
**1 teaspoon vanilla**
**1/2 cup dark raisins**

## DIRECTIONS:
Preheat oven to 350. Lightly butter a 9 x 13 inch baking dish. Place the bread or rolls in large mixing bowl and pour enough water over it to soak thoroughly, then let sit 15-20 minutes until water is absorbed. Mash the bread fine, and then use clean hands to gather and gently squeeze water out of bread. This sounds messy, but it's the way I made my bread pudding and it works. Return bread to mixing bowl.

Add remaining ingredients except raisins and mix well. Stir in raisins last. Spoon batter into prepared pan and bake at 350 for 40 minutes, or until top is light golden brown and pudding is set-knife inserted in center should come out clean. Remove from oven and cool slightly. Serve warm with whipped cream. Makes 8 -10 servings.

Bread comes in so many varieties, shapes and sizes today that it's easy to become confused over measurements like 2 slices of bread. When these recipes were developed, they were based on a standard loaf of white or cinnamon raisin or other loaf bread which weighed a pound. This would mean that 2 slices of bread, cut into small cubes would equal one cup, if packed (pressed down firmly, not squashed hard). With today's giant loaves, if you used two slices of some breads, it would be more than this and make the pudding too firm.

# Sweetened Whipped Cream

*This is another very easy thing to make, much better than canned or frozen toppings.*

1 cup cold whipping cream
2 tablespoons sifted confectioner's sugar
½ teaspoon vanilla, rum or other flavoring, if desired

Chill a deep small bowl, then combine ingredients in bowl and beat on high speed until as cream forms peaks as thick as desired.

# Cleo's Cheesecake

*When I first learned about this dessert, I thought all cheesecake came from New York City. I had some guests whose opinion was "of course it does! There is no other kind but New York cheesecake!" Cream cheese was not a thing we Caymanians cooked with until modern supermarkets made it available here. But today, it is a favorite dessert in Cayman. If I were making it for guests today, I would add 1 tablespoon grated key lime peel to this recipe and top it with stewed guava or mango. Years ago, glaze made from canned cherries had to do.*

### CRUST:
1-1/2 cups crisp breadcrumbs or crushed vanilla wafer crumbs
6 tablespoons butter or margarine, melted
3 tablespoons sugar
¼ teaspoon cinnamon

### FILLING:
5 8-ounce packages cream cheese, at room temperature
1-3/4 cups sugar
3 tablespoons flour
2 teaspoons vanilla extract
1 tablespoon grated key lime peel (optional)
5 large eggs
2 egg yolks
6 tablespoons heavy cream
Cherry glaze
1-15 ounce can tart pitted cherries
½ cup sugar
2 tablespoons cornstarch
2 drops red food coloring

**INGREDIENTS:**

**Make the crust:** Preheat oven to 375 F. Lightly butter the inside bottom of a 9-inch springform pan. Wrap the bottom and sides tightly with two layers of heavy foil so it cannot leak. In a small bowl, combine all ingredients with a fork until moistened and well mixed. Spread the mixture evenly over the bottom of greased pan, Use the bottom of a drinking glass, or your fingers, to firmly press down crust over bottom and about a half inch up the sides of the pan. Bake 10 minutes, or until crust is lightly browned and firm to the touch.

**Make the filling:** In large mixing bowl, use electric mixer to beat cream cheese until light and creamy, about 2 minutes, scraping the sides of bowl with a rubber spatula. Gradually add the sugar and cream the mixture for 2 minutes, then add the flour. Beat 1 minute longer, until mixture is very smooth. On medium speed, blend in the vanilla and lime peel, then add the eggs, one at a time, then the egg yolks, scraping sides of bowl and beaters to blend all ingredients well. Use low speed to mix in the heavy cream, blending well.

Use spatula to spoon batter into prepared crust and smooth the top. Bake 55-60 minutes, until cake is set but center two inches still jiggles slightly. Remove from oven and run a sharp knife around the inside edge of crust. Refrigerate warm cake, uncovered, 8 hours or overnight.

**Make the glaze:** Drain the cherries well, reserving juice. Add enough water to juice to make 1 cup of liquid. In medium saucepan, combine sugar and cornstarch and blend with fork. Stir in the juice and cook over medium high heat, stirring constantly, until mixture thickens, about 2 minutes. Remove from heat and stir in the cherries. Cool completely before spreading over cheesecake. Or top individual slices with a spoonful of glaze.

*\* Make sure you don't have anything strong in the refrigerator that will taint the flavor of the cheesecake-like unwrapped onions or garlic, or leftovers not tightly sealed. It is best to store the cake uncovered until well chilled so moisture won't form on top and make it soggy.*

# Cleo's Bread Pudding for a Crowd

*If you bring this to a party or church event, you will make a lot of friends!*

## INGREDIENTS:
30 slices white bread or dinner rolls
6 cups white sugar
25 large eggs, lightly beaten
8 cups evaporated milk
1 teaspoon salt
2 teaspoons cinnamon
1 teaspoon nutmeg
2 tablespoons vanilla
1 pound dark raisins
1 pound butter or margarine, melted

## DIRECTIONS:
Preheat oven to 350F. Lightly butter a 14 x 21 inch baking pan. Place the bread or rolls in very large mixing bowl. Pour enough water over bread to soak thoroughly, then let sit 15-20 minutes until water is absorbed, then mash the bread fine. Use clean hands to gather and gently squeeze water out of bread. This sounds messy, but it's the way I made my bread pudding and it works. Return bread to mixing bowl.

Add remaining ingredients except raisins and mix well. Stir in raisins last. Spoon batter into prepared pan and bake at 350 for one hour and 30 minutes or until top is light golden brown and pudding is set. A knife inserted in center should come out clean. Remove from oven and cool slightly. Serve warm with whipped cream. Makes 25-30 servings.

# Apple Crisp

*You can use green mangoes in this recipe, or even raw cho-cho. Like the apples, the fruit must be peeled and seeds, or pit removed.*

**TOPPING:**
1/2 cup flour
1/2 cup sugar
½ teaspoon cinnamon
6 tablespoons butter, cut into pieces
1/3 cup old-fashioned rolled oats (not quick cooking or instant)

**FILLING:**
4 cups peeled and sliced Granny Smith or other tart apples (about 3 large apples)
1 tablespoon lemon juice
1/3 cup firmly packed brown sugar
1/2 teaspoon ground cinnamon
1 tablespoon all purpose flour

**DIRECTIONS:**
Preheat oven to 375 F. Butter an 8-inch square baking dish.

**For Topping:** Combine all the topping ingredients (flour, sugar, butter, and oats) in a food processor and process until the mixture is crumbly (looks like coarse meal) and there are no large pieces of butter visible. (This can also be done with two knives or your fingertips.) Set aside while you prepare the filling.

**For Filling:** Peel, core, and slice the apples into 1/4 inch thick pieces. Place in a large bowl and add the lemon juice, brown sugar, cinnamon and flour. Gently combine. Spread the apple mixture in prepared baking dish. Sprinkle the prepared topping evenly over the apples.

Bake for approximately 40-45 minutes or until the topping is lightly browned and the filling is bubbly. Remove from oven and place on a wire rack to cool for about 15 minutes before serving.

# Blueberry Imperial

*You might be tempted to take a shortcut by using canned blueberry pie filling-please don't. Fresh blueberries really make this recipe, but frozen berries will do. And, I don't know why graham cracker crust has become so popular. It must be because it's easy. I think the taste takes away from the filling in this and many other recipes. Use it if you want, but I always used breadcrumbs mixed with a little butter, sugar and cinnamon and it tasted delicious.*

## INGREDIENTS:
**Crust: (for a 9 inch square pan)**
1-1/2 cups dry breadcrumbs
4 tablespoons (1/4 cup) butter, melted
2 tablespoons white sugar
1 tablespoon brown sugar
¼ teaspoon cinnamon

## DIRECTIONS:
Preheat oven to 350F. Combine the crumbs, butter, sugars and cinnamon in a medium bowl and blend gently. Spoon into a 9-inch pie pan or baking dish and use the back of a spoon to press firmly against bottom of the pan. Bake 8 -10 minutes, but do not allow to over brown! Cool completely before filling.

## CREAM FILLING:
2/3 cup sugar
3 tablespoons cornstarch
½ teaspoon salt
3 cups cream (evaporated milk)
3 large egg yolks, lightly beaten
1 tablespoon butter
2 teaspoons vanilla

## DIRECTIONS:
In a medium saucepan, whisk together sugar, cornstarch and salt until blended. Gradually stir in cream. Over medium heat, cook the cream mixture, stirring constantly, until the mixture comes to a boil and thickens. Continue boiling for one minute, then remove from heat. Place beaten egg yolks in a small bowl and gradually stir in half of the hot cream mixture. Blend, then stir the egg mixture slowly back into remaining mixture in saucepan. Return pan to heat and bring to a boil, stirring constantly; boil one minute longer. Remove from heat and stir in the butter and vanilla. Let cool for 10 minutes, then spoon over prepared crust. While filling is cooling, make the topping.

## TOPPING:

**2 cups fresh or frozen blueberries**
**1-1/2 tablespoons cornstarch**
**1/4 cup sugar**
**¼ teaspoon cinnamon**
**1 tablespoon key lime juice**
**½ tablespoon butter, softened**

## DIRECTIONS:

Rinse fresh blueberries and pat dry. If using frozen be sure they are completely thawed; pat dry to remove excess water. In a medium saucepan, mash 1 cup of the blueberries, then stir in cornstarch, sugar, cinnamon and lime juice. Cook over medium low heat, stirring constantly, until mixture begins to bubble and thickens. Stir in remaining blueberries and butter and stir until just berries are coated, then remove from heat. Cool 15 minutes, then spread over cooled filling. Chill dessert several hours before serving and top each serving with whipped cream. Makes 8 servings, but count on guests wanting seconds and thirds and....

# Cleo's Famous Éclairs

*These were one of the favorite sweets of the Bergstrom children who grew up at Tortuga Club and ate their meals in my kitchen. I had to keep my eye on those children or the éclairs would disappear before dinner time for the guests. They take patience to make but aren't that hard. It was a surprise to find something like éclairs in East End 40 years ago!*

## INGREDIENTS:
### VANILLA CUSTARD FILLING:
3 tablespoons cornstarch
2/3 cup sugar
1/2 teaspoon salt
3 cups evaporated milk
3 egg yolks
1 tablespoon butter, softened
2 teaspoons vanilla

### PUFF PASTRY:
1/2 cup butter
1 cup water
1 cup flour
4 large eggs

### CHOCOLATE GLAZE:
1 ounce unsweetened chocolate
1 teaspoon butter
1 cup confectioner's sugar
2 tablespoons boiling water

## DIRECTIONS:
**Make the filling:** In medium saucepan, blend the cornstarch, sugar and salt with a fork. Place egg yolks in small bowl and beat lightly. Gradually stir in the milk and cook over low heat, stirring constantly, until mixture thickens. Boil one minute longer, then remove from heat. Whisk half the milk mixture into egg yolks then gradually blend into mixture in pan. Stirring constantly, cook until mixture returns to a boil, cook 1 minute longer, stirring, then remove from heat. Stir in butter and vanilla until blended. Let cool while you make the pastry.

**For the éclair pastry:** Preheat oven to 400 F. Have an ungreased baking sheet ready. In small saucepan, combine butter and water and bring to a full boil. Slowly add flour, stirring rapidly to prevent lumps. Reduce heat to low and stir dough rapidly for a minute or until it comes together in a ball. Remove from heat and beat in eggs one at a time and continue beating until dough is smooth. Measure dough by large spoonfuls onto baking sheet and shape into 12 oblong pieces, 4 inches long and 1 inch wide. Leave 3 inches between éclairs. Bake 45-50 minutes or until puffed golden and dry. Cool on wire racks away from drafts. Using a sharp knife, carefully slice the top off each pastry and scoop out the soft dough. Using a small spoon, fill each with cooled custard filling and replace top. Lightly glaze with chocolate glaze.

**Chocolate glaze:** In small saucepan, combine chocolate and butter and melt over low heat, stirring frequently until mixed and smooth. Remove from heat and gradually stir in the sugar and enough hot water to make a smooth glaze. Spread glaze along the top of each éclair. Refrigerate éclairs on making sheet or plate lined with wax paper until ready to serve.

# Old Time Coconut Bars

*Everywhere she goes, Miss Cleo takes her Hospitality Ambassador from East End role seriously, greeting strangers and tourists in the street like old friends-and her real friends seem to be everywhere. One morning while at her bank in George Town, a well dressed young Caymanian businesswoman rushed to greet Cleo-it was a former Sunday Schools student from many years ago.*

*"Oh Miss Cleo, I remember those wonderful coconut bars you used to make for us at Sunday School! I wish someone made those today!" she said.*

I don't really remember this one in particular, but I made a lot of things years ago for the children. This is an old recipe and is probably the one my friend remembers.

### CRUST:
1 cup margarine or butter, at room
   temperature
1 cup brown sugar, firmly packed
2 cups flour

### TOPPING:
4 large eggs
¼ teaspoon salt
2 cups brown sugar, firmly packed
2 teaspoons vanilla extract
¼ cup flour
1 teaspoon baking powder
4 cups shredded or grated coconut,
   divided

### DIRECTIONS:
Preheat oven to 325 F. Lightly grease a 9 x 13 inch baking dish or pan. In a large mixing bowl, combine crust ingredients and blend well, about 2 minutes with an electric mixer. Press mixture evenly onto bottom of prepared pan and bake for 20 minutes, until very pale golden but not brown. Remove from oven and cool while making the topping.

In medium mixing bowl, combine all topping ingredients except coconut and mix until light, about 2 minutes on medium speed of electric mixer. Stir in 2 cups of coconut and spread mixture evenly over crust. Sprinkle with remaining coconut and bake at 325 for 25 minutes, until top is golden brown. Remove from oven and cool 10 minutes, then cut into small bars while still warm. Allow bars to cool completely in pan.

# Cleo's Gingerbread

*No one makes this wonderful dish anymore. I think most children today have grown up without ever tasting a piece of warm, homemade gingerbread. Once you make it, you can be sure your family will ask for it over and over again. It is best served warm with a little whipped cream on top.*

**INGREDIENTS:**
2-1/4 cups flour
1 teaspoon baking soda
1-1/2 teaspoons ground ginger
1 teaspoon cinnamon
½ teaspoon salt

½ cup butter, at room temperature
1/3 cup sugar
1 cup dark molasses
1 large egg, beaten
3/4 cup boiling water

**INGREDIENTS:**
Preheat oven to 325 F. Lightly grease and flour a 9 x 9 inch baking pan. In a medium bowl, mix together the dry ingredients (flour through salt) until blended. In a large mixing bowl, blend the butter and sugar until smooth, and then add the egg. Stir in molasses and water, blending well. Add flour mixture and beat mixture until smooth (about 2 minutes on medium speed of electric mixer.) Pour into prepared pan and bake for 45-50 minutes, or until wooden pick inserted in center comes out clean.

# Gelatin Desserts

When it was very hot I would sometimes make a simple dessert of Jell-O but I would top it with ice cream. That went over well with guests and I wondered if the combination was new and unusual to them. I think people have forgotten about gelatin desserts today, with so many fancy sweets ready to buy. But these old time recipes made delicious desserts.

# Pineapple Lime Cloud

*You can use lemon juice if you want, or half and half. Our Cayman limes make the best recipe, but today, after Ivan, it's hard to find enough to cook with. And you need to use fresh lime or lemon to get the grated peel.*

### INGREDIENTS:
1 -14.5 ounce can cream (evaporated milk)
1 -20 ounce can crushed pineapple
1 3 ounce box lemon flavored Jell-O
1 cup boiling water
¾ cup cold water & reserved pineapple juice combined
2 cups graham cracker or vanilla wafer crumbs
3 tablespoons sugar
1/2 cup grated or flaked coconut
2 tablespoons lime juice
1 tablespoon grated lime peel

### DIRECTIONS:
Put the cream (evaporated milk) in the freezer for 2 hours, until it barely sloshes when you shake the can. Do not freeze! Drain pineapple very well, reserving juice. Add enough water to juice to make ¾ cup and chill until cold.

Make Jell-O using 1 cup boiling water and the ¾ cup cold water/ juice combination, and chill until it thickens slightly, to the consistency of unbeaten egg whites.
Spray a 9 x 13 inch baking dish lightly with Pam spray. Combine crumbs, sugar and coconut and set aside ½ cup. Spread remaining crumb mixture evenly over bottom of baking dish. (OR you can use 2- 8 inch pie pans.)

Pour the half-frozen cream into medium bowl and use electric mixer to beat on high until milk forms soft peaks. Beat in the lime juice and peel. Beat Jell-O on high speed until fluffy, then fold into whipped cream. Fold in drained pineapple. Spoon into prepared pan and sprinkle with remaining crumb mixture. Chill 4-6 hours, or overnight. Makes about 10-12 servings.

# Snow Pudding

*This is an old recipe that is a light dessert and especially good in our summer heat. No one makes it today because it uses raw egg whites, but this never made anyone sick back then. However, if you don't eat anything with uncooked eggs, then you should skip this recipe. And that would be a shame. (Some may not be able to make this because modern kitchens don't have old fashioned hand rotary beaters!)*

### INGREDIENTS:
2 tablespoons (2 envelopes)
    unflavored gelatin
1-1/2 cups sugar
2-1/2 cups water
½ cup fresh lime juice
2 tablespoons grated lime peel
4 large egg whites

### SOFT CUSTARD SAUCE:
4 egg yolks
¼ cup sugar
¼ teaspoon salt
1-1/2 cups cream
    (evaporated milk)
1 teaspoon vanilla

### DIRECTIONS:
In a small saucepan, combine the gelatin, sugar and water and stir well to mix. Over medium high heat, bring mixture just to a boil, stirring constantly, then remove from heat. Stir in the lime juice and grated peel until blended. Refrigerate 30 minutes, or until mixture thickens enough to mound when dropped from a spoon. In a medium bowl, beat egg whites with rotary hand beater until they form stiff peaks. Very slowly fold egg whites in the gelatin mixture, just until blended, then use a rubber spatula to divide among 6 dessert dishes. Chill until firm, at least four hours. Serve with soft custard sauce.

**Soft custard sauce:**

Beat egg yolks in small bowl until thick and smooth. Add sugar and salt and blend well. Transfer egg mixture to the top of double boiler and gradually stir in cream, blending well. Place double boiler pan over simmering, not boiling water (water should not touch the bottom of top pan you are using) and cook, stirring constantly with a large spoon, until custard coats spoon with a thin layer. Remove from heat and blend in vanilla. Cool until just warm and serve on top of Snow Pudding.

# Glossary and Index

# Ingredients & Measures

Many island visitors are not familiar with the common seasonings and tropical ingredients we take for granted. Here are some of the most common ones, with tips on how to use them or make substitutions if appropriate.

### Coconut

See The Amazing Coconut chapter for complete information about this key island ingredient, including how to make fresh coconut milk.

### Thyme

One of the most common herbs used in Caribbean cooking, thyme remains an unfamiliar seasoning to many foreign cooks. Its pungent almost lemony-pepper flavor is easy to recognize once you know it. You probably won't be able to find fresh thyme, the preferred seasoning, but a teaspoon of dried thyme provides about the same flavoring as a large fresh sprig.

### Scallions (or escallions)

Also known as green onions or spring onions, scallions are another important Caribbean seasoning found in supermarkets worldwide. After cutting off the roots and removing the paper-like outer skin, chop and use the entire scallion in recipes, not just the white part.

### Ginger

Fresh gingerroot from Jamaica is available in the produce section of Cayman's supermarkets. It should have a smooth skin and pale buff or tan color. Use a vegetable peeler to peel away the thin skin and then grate, slice or mince to use in recipes. Cooks also disagree on the proper amount of powdered ground ginger to substitute for fresh grated ginger-it varies from 1/4 teaspoon to 1 teaspoon powdered ground ginger for 1 tablespoon grated fresh ginger. The flavors are very different anyway, so I don't advise you to substitute one for the other unless the recipe states this. A little ginger helps eliminate the fishy taste when added to fish soups and seafood chowders. Ginger tea is a remedy for head colds, bronchitis-and upset stomachs. And, many islanders swear ginger beer can help cure a hangover-fishermen and sailors stock ginger beer or ginger ale in coolers in case of seasickness.

### Curry Powder

Caymanians, Jamaicans and many West Indians generally like their curry spicy rich and "flavorful," but not fiery hot, and add Scotch Bonnets or other local hot pepper or hot sauce to the curry to suit individual taste. Jamaican and Trinidadian curry powders are now widely available in Cayman. One good variety is Trinidad's Chief Curry Powder, which contains a very flavorful combination of spices, nicely balanced with hot pepper.

### Nature's Seasons Seasoning (Morton's)

This blend of spices comes from the United States and has become a popular seasoning in Cayman. It is sold in the spice sections of supermarkets throughout Cayman.

### Browning

Browning is similar to Kitchen Bouquet® and Gravy Master® and sold in 5-ounce bottles and an important, versatile ingredient in Caribbean cooking. You can find it in any Caribbean supermarket, from Trinidad to Grand Cayman, and in many foreign supermarkets. This caramelized sugar-based flavoring is frequently used in soups, stews and meat dishes as well as sauces and gravies. Use either of the other products if you can't find browning.

### Evaporated and Condensed Milk

Evaporated milk and sweetened condensed milk are common ingredients in Caribbean cooking, but they are not the same thing and not interchangeable. Evaporated milk is unsweetened milk with 40% of the water removed, often used in place of cream on the table or in recipes. Mix equal parts water and evaporated milk as a substitute for the same measure of regular milk. Sweetened condensed milk, invented around 1860, has half the water of whole milk and a lot of sugar. A 14-ounce can contains the fat equivalent of 2-1/2 cups milk, before the water is removed, and ½ cup sugar. It is used in baking as a sauce or sweetener in place of cream and sugar combined.

### Thickeners for Gravy or Sauces

If your sauce, stew or gravy is not thick enough and you're afraid you won't have enough of it if you reduce it by boiling longer, use flour or cornstarch to thicken.

**The rule of thumb:** 1 tablespoon cornstarch will thicken 2 cups liquid. Mix either with a tablespoon or two of cold water to make a paste, then stir into the sauce. Cook over low heat to remove any starchy flavor and thicken the sauce.

You can also use flour, mixing one part flour to two parts water or stock to form a paste. Use about the same proportion as cornstarch-1 tablespoon will thicken 2 cups but you must cook the sauce or stew at least three minutes after adding the flour paste, stirring with a wire whisk, to blend smoothly and avoid lumps, to cook out the raw floury taste.

Adding peeled and sliced breadfruit to stews and soups will also help thicken the broth but this requires longer cooking.

# Weights and Measures

**Liquid measures (US):**

| | |
|---|---|
| 3 teaspoons | 1 tablespoon |
| 1 tablespoon | ½ fluid ounce (oz.) |
| 2 tablespoons | 1 fluid ounce or 1/8 cup |
| 4 tablespoons | 2 fluid ounces or ¼ cup |
| 8 tablespoons | 4 fluid ounces or ½ cup |
| 16 tablespoons | 8 fluid ounces or 1 cup |
| 1 cup | ½ pint or 8 fluid ounces |
| 1 pint | 2 cups or 16 fluid ounces |
| 1 quart | 4 cups or 32 fluid ounces |
| 1 gallon | 4 quarts or 128 fluid ounces |

**Liquid measures (UK):**

| | |
|---|---|
| 1 Imperial pint | 20 ounces |
| ½ pint | 10 ounces |
| ¼ pint | 5 ounces |
| 1 Imperial quart | 40 ounces or 4.227 cups |
| 1 Imperial Gallon | 160 ounces |

**Dry measures:**

| | |
|---|---|
| "Pinch" | a scant 1/8 teaspoon |
| 1 teaspoon | 1/3 tablespoon |
| 3 teaspoons | 1 tablespoon |
| 1 dessertspoon | 1 scant tablespoon |
| ½ tablespoon | ½ ounce |
| 2 tablespoons | 1 ounce |
| 4 tablespoons | 2 ounces or ¼ cup |
| 8 tablespoons | 4 ounces or ½ cup |
| 12 tablespoons | 6 ounces or ¾ cup |
| 16 tablespoons | 8 ounces or 1 cup |

**Dry Ingredient Measures:**

| | |
|---|---|
| 1 pound granulated sugar | 2 cups |
| 1 pound brown sugar | 2-1/4 cups packed |
| 1 pound powdered sugar | 3-1/2 cups |
| 1 cup honey | 1-1/4 cups white sugar plus ¼ cup liquid |
| 1 pound all purpose flour | 3-1/2 cups |
| 1 pound rice | 2 cups dry, or 4 cups cooked |
| 1 pound loaf bread | 12-16 slices |
| 1 cup soft breadcrumbs | 1-1/2- 2 slices bread |

**Dairy and canned milk products:**

| | |
|---|---|
| 1 pound butter or margarine | 2 cups or 4 sticks |
| ½ pound butter | 1 cup or 2 sticks |
| ¼ pound butter | ½ c or 1 stick, or 8 Tablespoon |
| 1 –13 ounce can evaporated milk | 1-2/3 cups |
| 1- 14 ounce can condensed milk | 1-1/4 cups |
| 1 cup heavy cream | 2 cups whipped cream |
| 1 14-ounce can coconut milk | 1-3/4 cups |

**Fruits and vegetables:**

| | |
|---|---|
| 1 pound bananas | 3 medium |
| 1 pound apple bananas | 8-10- 3-inch fruits |
| 1 pound dry beans, red | 2-1/2 cups dry or 6 cups cooked |
| 1- 3 pound fit breadfruit | 6 cups, peeled & diced |
| 1 pound carrots | 3 cups grated |
| 1 average brown coconut | -1/2 pounds, 3 -3-1/2 cups coarse grated meat |
| 1 average brown coconut | ½ - 1 cup coconut water |
| 1 average green coconut | 2-3 cups coconut water, plus jelly |
| 2 medium ears corn | 1 cup kernels |
| 1-1/2 inch piece* gingerroot | 1 ounce or about 1-1/2 tablespoons grated (*called a "thumb") |
| 1 medium green pepper | 1 cup chopped (seeded and cored) |
| 1 medium lemon | 2-3 tablespoons juice, 1-1/2 -2 teaspoons grated peel |
| 1 medium Persian lime | 2-3 tablespoons juice, 1-1/2 – 2 teaspoons grated peel |
| 1 key lime | 2 –3 teaspoons juice, ¾-1 teaspoon grated peel |
| 1 medium mango | ¾ to 1 pound, 1-1/2 cups peeled and diced, 1 cup puree |
| 1 large mango | 1-1/2 pounds, 2-1/2 cups peeled and diced, 2 cups puree |
| 1 medium onion | 1 cup chopped |
| 1 large onion | 2-1/2 -3 cups chopped |
| 1 medium orange | 1/3-cup juice, 2 –2-1/2 tablespoons grated peel |
| 1 pound peaches | 3 large, about 1- 1-1/2 cups sliced |
| 1 medium pumpkin (calabaza) | 5 pounds or about 4-1/2 cups cooked mashed |
| 1 large soursop | 1 quart pulp, seeds removed |
| 1 quart strawberries | 4 cups hulled berries |
| 1 pound tomatoes | 2 large ripe (3 inches in diameter) or 3 medium |
| 3 medium white potatoes | 2 cups peeled and diced |

**Seafood**

| | |
|---|---|
| 1 pound cleaned conch | 7-8 average or 4 large, 2- 2-1/4 cups ground |
| 1 pound Caribbean lobster | 2 medium (8 ounce) tails, including shell weight |
| 1 pound shrimp | 12-14 jumbo; 21-30 large; 31-40 medium |

# Recipe Index

## A

avocado (pear)
    Avocado Soup, 90

## B

bananas
    Banana Nut Bread, 74-75
    Banana Cream Pie, 177-178
    Cayman Coconut Banana Bread, 75
    Hawaiian Banana Pie, 182

barbecue
    fish, 125
    sauces, 125, 169

beef
    Beef Beaujolais (Bourguignon), 148
    Cleo's Meatloaf, 150
Corned Beef & Cabbage, 149
Cowfoot, 38
Old Fashioned Beef Stew, 146
Oven Baked Beef Roast, 153
    Pepper Steak, 156
Pot Roast with Tomato Gravy, 147
Steak & Kidney Pie, 152-153
Swiss Steak, 155
Sukiyaki, 154

beets
    Beets in Orange Sauce (Royal Beets), 99

breads
    Banana Nut Bread, 74-75
    Biscuits, Old Time, 72
    Cayman Coconut Banana Bread, 75
    Cheese Garlic Biscuits, 73
    Cleo's Cayman Style Cornbread, 65
    Cleo's Cheese Nut Bread, 74
    Cleo's Corn Muffins for 150, 66
    Cleo's Quick Sally Lunn, 69
    Herb Bread, 70

Johnny cakes, 28
Onion Bread, 72-73
Pineapple Bread, 76
Popovers, 67
Sensational Egg Bread, 71
Simple English Scones, 64
Yorkshire Pudding, 68

breadfruit
    Breadfruit Chips,
    Breadfruit Salad, 94
    Breadfruit Scallops, 95

bread pudding (see Desserts)

browning (seasoning), 206

## C

cakes (see also desserts)

    Cleo's Cheesecake, 191-192
    Cleo's Prize Lemon Cake, 188
    Coconut Pound Cake, 187
    Harris Griffiths Conolly's Christmas
    Fruit Cake, 43-44
    Pineapple Upside Down Cake, 42-43

cassava
    Frank Conolly's Cassava Heavy Cake, 52-53

Caymanian cookery
    Baked Crab, 33
    Breadfruit Salad, 94
    Cayman Pepper Sauce, 169
    Conch Chowder, Red, 110
    Conch Chowder, East End style, 108-109
    Cowfoot, 38
    Macaroni & Cheese, 93
    Marinated Conch, 108
    Cole Slaw (Salad), 31
    Cornmeal Custard, 39
    Coconut Cream (Coconut Jello), 41